A MINISTER'S WIFE GOES ROGUE

Releasing Religion

A Memoir

Gaye Kick

PALANCA PRESS

Palanca Press
Springfield, IL

ISBN
979-8-9884244-0-6   ebook
979-8-9884244-1-3   paperback

Library of Congress Control Number: 2023909670

First Edition
Book Production and Publishing by Brands Through Books
brandsthroughbooks.com

www.gayellenkick.com

Releasing
Religion

"Page-turner" might seem like an overused term for a book. But when it comes to this meaningful and complex story that is told with such honesty and heart, you can't help but to turn the page!

—CASEY HUTCHISON, creator/writer of award-winning audio soap opera *Forever and a Day*

A whiplash of a narrative—hilarious highs and heartfelt lows, interspersed with Gaye's own brand of fun and humor. You'll enjoy this lady's journey into herself and how she comes out as a fully functional, happy, new person.

—KEN MITCHELL, author of eighteen books, including local bestseller *North-End Pride*

Served up with humor, candor, and a surprising dash of the unexpected, this minister wife's story may inspire you to examine and release some old ideas of your own.

—CRYSTAL HODGE, contributing writer to the *Chicken Soup for the Soul®* series

Gaye shares her unexpected life path with such grace, insight, and humor, you'll be inspired to start (or finish) your own spiritual journey! No matter life's twists and turns, she shows that we all have the ability to find our peace and connect with our highest potential.

—ALYSSA FURLING, restaurant and real estate entrepreneur

Reading Gaye's book is truly enjoyable. Her sincere and humorous writing style combines perfectly with her personal and spiritual journey, resulting in a heartwarming read with themes that resonate and leave a lasting impression.

—JYLL HOYRUP, intuitive energy healer and author of *Rock Your Intuition*

To my parents,

Dorothy and Richard Zimmermann,

with love

Contents

Introduction

I NEVER ANTICIPATED MY SPIRITUAL JOURNEY would expand beyond my traditional religious upbringing. Unable to explain this spiritual expansion to my family and friends, I hid the truth out of fear of what they would think and concern that they would worry about me.

Oh, No! She's gone off the deep end! She won't be with us in heaven! We must save her!

Hiding my true self caused feelings of guilt about being secretive. I couldn't share the most important aspect of my life with people I knew and loved, so I clenched my teeth, silenced my voice, and put on a plastic smile. And then, longing to live authentically, I realized that my compulsion to avoid disappointing others put me at the mercy of their wishes.

If you fear what others think of you, believe you aren't good enough for your dreams to come true, take care of the needs of others but not your own, are not embracing that you are the only authority over what is best for you, and are discouraged with traditional religion but still want a connection to the spirit world, this book is for you!

Life happens for us. We can't get it wrong.

—*Gaye Kick*

PART ONE

Losing Myself

In Over My Head

*"If you don't design your own life plan, chances
are you'll fall into someone else's."*
—JIM ROHN

READY TO DISCOVER MY PLACE IN the WORLD, I headed to college
at eighteen, equipped with a teacher's grant, a music scholarship, and a goal to become a public school music teacher. I had
a plan, and nothing was going to stop me from fulfilling it.

Nevertheless, during that year, I lost focus, and when I
came to my senses, I had a supporting role in somebody else's
plan. *Ugh!*

~ FALL 1971 ~

Four rows of empty folding chairs stood in a semicircle facing the conductor's music stand, where I stood in the Illinois
State University music room with my three girlfriends from
high school. We quietly conversed with the other newbie first-
year students who had auditioned the previous week and made
the concert choir cut.

The returning choir members assembled at the back of
the room, freely joking around as one would with friends they
hadn't seen all summer. One student was hard to miss when he
entered the room. His infectious laugh and boisterous energy

3

commanded attention. All the freshmen stopped talking to watch him. His thick black hair, spindly goatee, rumpled T-shirt, and six-foot-two thin frame reminded me of Shaggy from the Hanna-Barbera *Scooby-Doo* cartoon. He was the worst-dressed student in the room, yet he didn't seem to care. I found that intriguing.

The professor was all business when he walked into the room shouting commands. "Sopranos! Front two rows on my right. Altos! Front two rows on my left. Basses behind sopranos. Tenors behind altos."

As I found a place to sit with the sopranos, I glanced behind me to see which section Shaggy was in before I sat down. He smiled directly at me from the tenor section.

Oh my gosh!

Flustered, I plunked down on my chair, plastering my eyes on the conductor, reasoning that Shaggy must have been looking at the girl next to me. After all, why would an older college student pick me out of a crowd?

The choir was scheduled to sing the "Star-Spangled Banner" and the school's alma mater at the ISU Redbird football game the following evening. After introductions, distributing the music, and receiving instructions for the football gig, there was only time to run through the songs a few times. I considered going to one of the practice rooms later that day to run through the alma mater again.

After class, I said goodbye to my girlfriends, Chris, Doreen, and Gayle, and had just grabbed my purse from under the chair when Shaggy approached, towering over my five-foot-four, one-hundred-five-pound body by ten inches.

"Welcome to ISU! My name's Donn. I'm a senior music major. What's your name?"

Yikes! He had been looking at me.

Grinning, I replied, "My name's Gaye. Soprano. Freshman music major."

"Hello, Gaye. I'm going to the practice rooms to run through the alma mater. You can join me if you don't have to get to another class."

Had he read my mind?

"Sure. I was just heading there," I lied.

I don't usually go into a closed room with a boy I'd just met, but I'd scouted out the practice rooms several days earlier and knew they had a long narrow window in each door.

As we walked down the hallway, he commented, "I like your hair. It's different."

Three months earlier, at new-student orientation, I realized I was one of a sea of girls with long dark brown wavy hair. For the first time, I didn't want to look like everyone else. When I got back home, I had my hair cut into a short shag—a layered unisex style worn by my older sister, Melody, and celebrities like actors Jane Fonda, who starred in *Klute* in 1971, and David Cassidy, the heartthrob of the *Partridge Family* TV show. Apparently, my new hairdo did set me apart from other girls.

When we found an empty practice room, Donn asked, "Do you want to play the accompaniment, or should I?"

I wasn't confident enough in my piano skill to sight-read a new song in front of a guy. I played for enjoyment and to learn my vocal parts. At one time, I considered becoming a concert pianist, but I laid that dream to rest when I realized I would have to practice scales, which I hated.

"No, you go right ahead."

Donn had an incredible singing voice. His high tenor with my trained high soprano blended well, and his piano playing blew me away. It was energetic, seizing attention, just like his personality. We were both going to be music teachers. Musically, we had a lot in common, and we started dating that evening.

Every afternoon when his classes were finished, he headed to his part-time job cleaning the print shop at the United Methodist Central Illinois Conference office on the campus of Wesleyan University in Bloomington. It was a two-minute drive from ISU's campus in Normal.

He also had a part-time Sunday night job as the youth leader at a United Methodist Church twenty-five miles away. I went with him several times, but all I did was stand around, feeling awkward as he interacted with the teens. Some were just a year younger than me.

Since I wasn't one of the kids or a leader, I felt out of place. I was just a tag-along with no reason to be there other than my dorm's cafeteria didn't serve meals on Sunday night, and he'd buy me a burger on the way to church. Don't judge me. A girl has to eat.

During the spring semester of 1972, before his graduation in May, Donn was off campus for his student teaching. He was now clean-shaven, with short hair and wearing nice clothing, the model of tall, dark, and handsome.

We never discussed what would happen to our relationship after he graduated, and then, after knowing me for only six months, he proposed in early March. All I remember about the moment is the stipulation that I had to marry him in June. If I didn't, our relationship would be over. He wasn't going to date someone in college.

My reaction to the proposal was not a gushing "Yes, I can't live without you!" I was a romantic without much real-world experience who dated occasionally but rarely had a steady boyfriend. When I did, it didn't last longer than a few months. I was flattered that a senior in college wanted to marry me, but I couldn't think straight with a wedding expiration date hanging over my head like a guillotine.

Our relationship wasn't awful, but it wasn't fantastic either. I often had niggles of doubt and tried to break up with him several times, but I'd cave when I looked into his sad brown eyes.

Then, in a moment of clarity, my plan to teach music arose from the tornado in my head. "What about my college degree?"

He came right back with, "You can go to school anywhere. It doesn't have to be at ISU unless I get a teaching job in this area."

He was right; I could finish school elsewhere. Although still hesitant, I agreed to the proposal but did not tell my parents.

The following morning, before concert choir, I showed my engagement ring to my girlfriends from high school. They were surprised but appeared to be genuinely happy for me. When I stepped off the elevator onto my dorm floor later in the day, I heard the persistent ring of a wall phone coming from one of the rooms. It was mine. I quickly unlocked the door and picked up the receiver.

"YOU'RE ENGAGED?" My mother hollered.

Oh, crap!

My friend Gayle had called her mother, who immediately called my mother. Mom was devastated that she didn't hear the news from me and over-the-top furious that I'd said yes.

"You hardly know this guy! You don't want to give up college for a boy! What's the rush? He's pushing you into this because he's graduating in three months and wants a wife."

After the admonishment on the phone, more doubts about the engagement grew exponentially as Mom's words swirled through my mind. I desperately needed guidance to quell my state of panic.

When my parents dropped me off at college in September, my dad gave me a Bible and said, "Use it when you need guidance." It was a black hardcover four-and-a-half by eight-inch *Good News for Modern Man* New Testament written in today's English. It was about time someone put the Bible into modern language that people could understand. No more stumbling over the King James Bible with its seventeenth-century vocabulary—*Verily, verily I say unto thee, thou hast hurt thine mother, deeply.*

After the phone call, I grabbed the New Testament from my dorm room shelf. I'd memorized all the books of the Bible at the age of thirteen, along with thirty-five other students whose parents were Lutheran and sent their kids to confirmation classes. We spent every Saturday morning at church with the minister, memorizing a bunch of useless information so we could legally drink those tiny cups of communion wine once a month at church.

Sadly, they didn't teach us anything about wine. We had to learn that on our own in high school. I recommend not drinking a bottle of Boone's Farm strawberry wine on Saturday night if you'll be sitting in the church choir loft three feet from the smell of two hundred cups of wine the following morning.

What I didn't receive during this instruction was practical application about where to go in the Bible to find direction. I opened the gift from my father to the first chapter of the book of Matthew.

You're supposed to start at the beginning of a book. I was taught that in school.

Instead of words of wisdom, I found these: *This is the record of the genealogy of Jesus Christ, the son of David, the son of Abraham.*

*Abraham was the father of Isaac, Issac the father of Jacob, Jacob the father of Judah and his brothers, Judah the father of...*and on and on it went until I got to the story of Jesus' birth, which I knew by heart because I'd either participated in or watched all the church Christmas pageants since the age of three. Discouraged, I tossed the New Testament back on the shelf.

I didn't know what to do. Desperate, I turned to my roommate for advice, which was weird because we barely spoke even though we lived together in a space the size of a jail cell. *Not that I've ever been in jail.*

I don't remember her name, but I do remember that she was bossy. The first week of school, she wanted us to shop for matching bedspreads and an area rug but wouldn't listen to my input even though I was paying half the cost.

The rug she picked was so cheap that my socks stuck to it like Velcro every time I walked across the room. The bedspreads she insisted we buy were covered with large, colorful, cartoonish animals. Our room looked like it belonged to two five-year-olds.

She wasn't the best person to ask for advice, for she was also engaged to a guy three years older. He lived two hours away. She would skip her Friday classes to take the train home for the weekend, not returning until late Sunday. By the end of the school year, she didn't return until late Monday or early Tuesday.

When I told her I was considering returning the ring and breaking up with Donn, she yelled at me, "That's just cruel. How could you even consider doing such a thing? Don't let your parents make that decision for you."

Her reprimand made me think of David, whom I dated during the summer between my junior and senior high school years. I don't count him as a steady boyfriend because it was just a summer fling, and he wasn't from my town or school, where I still consider myself semi-dateless.

David was a cute blonde from South Dakota who drove a baby blue Mustang hatchback. He had just graduated from high school, moved into the area, and worked at the Admiral plant in my hometown, Harvard, Illinois, where I made television sets at my summer job. We met in June, and I was wearing his class ring by mid-July.

My father didn't like David. His excuse was that he didn't come to the door to pick me up, and his car was always dirty. It was an odd comment, considering Dad built houses for a living, and his truck was always muddy from construction sites.

Mom didn't like David either. He was a year older than me and lived alone in a tiny one-bedroom rental house seven miles away in Wisconsin, just across the Illinois border. My parents were probably concerned I would be hanging out in his bedroom, but I wasn't that kind of girl.

I went to his house once for five minutes when he needed to grab a jacket. I saw the dirty dishes stacked all over his kitchen, the overflowing garbage can, and crumpled clothes scattered everywhere. I couldn't get out fast enough.

"Nice place," I lied. "I'll wait for you outside."

I liked David a lot, but I didn't want tension with my parents, plus I was entering my senior year in a few weeks. I needed a boyfriend from my school so I would have a date for the homecoming dance and prom.

Fingers crossed!

When my summer job ended in August, we sat in David's Mustang in front of my house, and I returned his ring. "I'm not allowed to date you anymore."

I kissed him goodbye and got out of the car. When I turned around to look at him one last time, his ring flew past my head and into the lawn. His last words were, "How much longer are you gonna let your parents run your life?"

I never saw him or the ring again, even though I spent hours the following day on my hands and knees combing through blades of grass, searching for it. And now, here I was again, asking myself the same question, "Whom should I disappoint, my parents or a guy?"

My mother's words still caused uncertainty about getting married. Still, it was surprisingly easy to ignore her voice when it was 150 miles away, especially when I had such a strong feeling that if I didn't marry Donn, I would miss something big. I had no idea what that might be, but I had to see where it would lead.

CHAPTER 2

Marriage Is for Life?

IN 1972, THERE WERE VERY FEW teaching jobs in Illinois, especially for music, but Donn did have an interview at a southwest Chicago school. I pictured us singing duets together in a cute little bungalow with a flower garden and white picket fence in the suburbs. I envisioned dropping Donn off at his teaching job, handing him his lunch, and heading to my college classes somewhere in the area.

Unfortunately, the position in Chicago didn't pan out. The school wanted a full-time teacher who could teach music and other subjects like math, science, or English. Donn's major and minor were both in music, instrumental and vocal.

Two weeks after the engagement, Donn received a phone call from a United Methodist District Superintendent. A part-time student pastorate position was open in his district if Donn was willing to attend seminary and pastor two churches an hour's drive south of Chicago, just off Route 66. Donn accepted the position without discussing it with me.

When he picked me up in his green Opal station wagon, he was bursting with excitement as he told me his *great* news. A sudden proposal and now a career change? What the hell?

"So, you're not going to be a teacher. You're going to be a—minister?"

My panicked, scrunched-up face must have been his clue that this news wasn't as thrilling for me as it was for him, for he explained without further prompt from me, "When I joined the church at the age of twelve, I felt called to become a local church pastor. So, in high school, I completed a course to become a certified lay speaker in the Methodist church. I planned to study theology at Illinois Wesleyan, but because of finances, I went to college in Springfield, majored in music, and taught at a music store. I became a licensed lay pastor in 1970 before I transferred to ISU. I'm sure I told you all this."

I knew he was certified to speak from the pulpit and, at one time, wanted to be a minister. I thought it was like me *once* wanting to be a concert pianist, then abandoning the idea—forever.

"I had no idea you still wanted to be a minister."

He hesitated momentarily, "I received the call from God but couldn't go to Wesleyan. It felt right to continue preparing for the church while studying music because I thought the two would fit together someday."

He took my hands in his. "You're so comfortable to be with. It feels like we've been together for a long time. Honestly, I thought you already knew I was doing both. This opportunity is a dream come true for me."

Yes, I should have seen this coming. Donn was a youth minister at a church. He worked at the conference office and continuously talked about his experiences counseling at church camp every summer. He also planned and led a weekend youth rally that I attended. How could I have been so blind?

There was nothing I could do about Donn's sudden career change. I had just defied my parents and committed to marriage. Maybe this was the "something big" I would miss if we didn't marry.

"This isn't just about me," Donn added. "You're going to be a minister's wife."

Holy Moley!

I thought of my own minister and his wife. I could never imagine him lazing in a recliner, bare-chested, his shoes neglectfully tossed on the floor, watching TV like my dad. Nor could I picture his wife kneeling like my mom as she cleaned out the refrigerator with Trixie, the family dachshund lying across the back of her legs.

I'm only eighteen years old! Don't I need a direct line to God to be a minister's wife?

"Oh, I forgot to tell you," Donn added, his eyes sparkling. "We'll be living next door in the church parsonage. We won't have to pay rent!"

My own house?

Concern about marriage and being a clergy wife took a sudden 180-degree turn into fantasy. I saw that bungalow with a flower garden and a white picket fence. I saw Donn and me driving back and forth to Chicago to continue our higher education. I saw myself as the beloved minister's wife, standing quietly next to my husband, smiling and shaking hands as my minister's wife did.

Hmmm. I don't remember his wife ever speaking. Surely she did.

Donn applied to a seminary in Chicago. The school felt his liberal arts music degree didn't have the foundation he would need in seminary. They recommended that he take two basic courses at a junior college first, so he registered at Joliet Junior College, twenty-five miles north of where we would be living.

Unknown to me, when my dad came to pick me up for spring break, he pulled Donn aside. "Don't call. Don't write. Give her time to think this through."

When I arrived home, I thought Donn's soon-to-be new title would appease my parent's disapproval. In my teenager's mind, "minister's wife" was right up there with every mother's dream of her daughter becoming the wife of a doctor or lawyer. I couldn't have been more naïve.

Mom pulled me aside the first evening back home, saying, "We need to talk." I hopped onto the kitchen counter, pretending to be cool and relaxed. With her arms folded in front of her, Mom stood about four feet away, next to the built-in oven.

"If you realize that you've made a mistake after you get married, what will you do?"

The question took me by surprise. The divorce rate skyrocketed in the 1960s and 1970s. People everywhere were talking about it. I shrugged and quickly answered, "I'll get a divorce."

Mom's jaw took a dive off her face. "Gaye Ellen, marriage is for life!"

Marriage is for life? My brain went into overdrive.

Divorce was prevalent in the United States but not in our small town. None of my friends had divorced parents. My parents didn't have divorced friends. My family went to church every Sunday, but we weren't what I would call religious. However, the wedding vows did say, "Until death do us part."

Maybe marriage is for life! Hmmm.

The more she talked, the more I dug in my heels. The marriage concerns I'd buried under the fantasy bungalow and picket fence were now blooming in the flower garden of fear. I'd already made a commitment to Donn. If marriage were for life, I would have to do everything I could to make it work and prove my mother wrong. The next day, I had an unanticipated appointment to see our minister.

I've given this meeting a lot of thought over the years. I might have come clean if he had said something like, "Everyone has doubts before they get married. Let's talk about yours, so you know for sure this is what you really want. And if it isn't, I can help you figure out the best way to tell him." But he didn't say anything supportive like that. His questions offered only yes or no answers, so I led him to believe I wanted to get hitched.

Even though they weren't thrilled, my parents accepted my decision. Mom and I picked out material for the wedding dresses. My older sister, Melody, sewed her own. Mom sewed my sister Julie's and finished my dress after I put the sleeves on backward.

My dad just wanted me to be happy. His only comment was, "I hope Donn likes fried egg sandwiches." It was his way of teasing me about my lack of culinary skills. Even now, I'd rather clean the kitchen than cook in it.

Over the years, I've looked back at how I ignored the pit in my stomach and the voice that whispered, "Don't go through with it," while at the same time insisting I wanted to get married. That girl only existed for those few months between the engagement and the wedding. Afterward, she returned to the comfortable, safe state of not making waves.

Back Story

WHEN MY MOTHER, DOTTIE, WAS FIVE years old, she dragged a chair over to the oven, pulled down the oven door, and pretended to play the piano. Although it was the 1930s and during the Great Depression, my grandparents scraped together enough money for piano lessons.

Unlike me, Mom practiced her scales rigorously. By the age of ten, she was already an accomplished pianist. In downtown Chicago, in the Gold Room of the Auditorium Building at 431 South Wabash Avenue, my mother's music teacher and a violin teacher held an evening recital for their two most outstanding students. The violinist played five memorized pieces, and according to the program, Mom played seven: "Solfeggietto" (Bach), "Waltz in C Major" (Schubert), "Sonata in C Major" (Mozart), "Chaconne" (Durand), "A Midsummer Day" (Courtney), "An Old Time Legend" (Barbour), and "The Butterfly" (Lavallée).

The piano became an important fixture in our home as Mom surrounded her three girls with love and live music. According to my baby book, the piano attracted me at an early age. "At six months, Gaye wiggles her way under the piano to suck on the pedals."

Ew!

We didn't just listen to music; we created it. "Gaye can sing songs at two and a half. Her favorites are 'Shortnin' Bread' and 'Jesus Loves Me.'" When I was three and Melody was five, we sang "O Tannenbaum" ("Oh Christmas Tree") at church. The older ladies would see us during the year and bend down to our level to inquire, "Are you the little girls who sing in German?"

"Yes, we are," Melody would reply. I didn't talk as much back then as I do now.

It was natural for us to sing in another language. The sounds I associated with family gatherings, which included my grandparents and great-grandparents, are an intermingling of the old and new world accents. Mom's father immigrated to the United States from Germany with his family at age five, and her mother's father immigrated from Norway.

One of my favorite memories of my musical mother is from when I was in elementary school. Late one rainy Saturday afternoon, I accompanied her to the church. She was subbing for the organist the following day and needed to run through the songs. As I was holding her hand in the dimly lit sanctuary, we hurried up the red carpet to the front of the church. I sat next to her on the pipe organ's bench as she turned it on, opened her music, and set the stops for her prelude. (Stops are drawbars, buttons, and tabs used to create many musical sound variations.)

I heard the organ many times on Sunday mornings. I had even heard Mom play, yet this time was special—I was by her side. I watched in awe as her eyes focused on the music, her fingers floated across the keys, and her feet played the pedals underneath the organ.

How did she make her hands, feet, and eyes work independently like that?

With the glow of the organ light illuminating our faces in the dark sanctuary, majestic harmonies filled the room and my soul.

* * *

I grew up with two sisters. The oldest, Melody, was the leader; she made up the rules. Julie, the youngest, was the rebel; she broke the rules. I was the follower, the pleaser, the peacekeeper.

Melody planned our daily activities: tea party, Old Maid, dress-up, and board games. She choreographed dance steps and created costumes for us to put on shows for our parents. When she was into sewing Barbie doll clothes, we put on fashion shows for the neighborhood. During intermission, I strolled along the runway (driveway) with an umbrella spinning on my shoulder, singing "Tip Toe through the Tulips" and "How Much is That Doggie in the Window."

Melody, my idol, was the smartest, most creative person I knew. Anything she believed, I believed, too. When she saw me reading a Nancy Drew book in the ninth grade, she said, "You're too old for Nancy Drew." She handed me the book she had just finished, *Desiree* by Annemarie Selinko, a 608-page book about Napoleon's first love.

Napoleon? Who's he?

The book was so far over my head I couldn't get past the first page. I held onto it for a month, then snuck it back onto her bookshelf. Not surprisingly, Melody's lifelong career has been as a high school history teacher.

The rebel, Julie, came along six years after me. Where I was the conformist, doing whatever was suggested by others, Julie wasn't about to be told what to do. She didn't have to change her bedsheets every week like the rest of us after she complained, "But Mom, it takes a whole week to get the sheets broken in!"

When she was eleven, and Melody was away at college, Julie got out of doing dishes by simply walking out of the kitchen, shouting over her shoulder, "I have homework." Mom didn't say a word, probably because I was already helping like I always did.

What happened to Mom's house rule, "When everyone works together, the work gets done faster"?

Julie's lifelong career has been in the airline industry, from ticket agent to station manager and everything in between. For the past two decades, she's been in customer service, handling passenger complaints for several airlines. You've probably talked to her if you've ever filed an airline grievance.

I was in awe of both my sisters. Melody, the creative, and Julie, the rebel. They both knew how to stand their ground. I aimed to be Pollyanna from the 1960 Disney movie of the same name, starring Hayley Mills. After losing the use of her legs in an accident, Pollyanna, the ultimate optimist, was still able to lift the spirits of an entire New England town.

What a gal!

Having no brothers, I was ignorant about boys. A few of them showed interest, but they were just friends. I didn't want to date them. The boys I liked didn't ask me out. Mom said they were afraid of me, although I couldn't imagine why. If anything, I was afraid of them.

When I was a sophomore in high school, my dad bought me a book for Christmas, *How to Get a Teen-Age Boy and What to Do with Him When You Get Him*. Sadly, it wasn't helpful.

I was never on the homecoming or prom court, even though I'd been a cheerleader for six years. Maybe it was the cheerleading thing that scared the boys, or perhaps I came across as a goody-two-shoes because I didn't sleep around.

Since I wasn't dating regularly, I filled my time with music, starting with the piano in the third grade and a twenty-six-inch clarinet with a smelly case that my parents bought used in the fifth grade. In the eleventh grade, I switched to a school-owned forty-inch bass clarinet with a silver bell at the bottom and a curved neck at the top. Its sensual deep bass notes were so beautiful that sometimes I would get the shivers. *Yum.*

In high school, Melody and I took classical singing lessons. Mom would leave work early on Tuesday, pick us up after school, and drive forty miles to the Mendelssohn Club in downtown Rockford for lessons. (It's now called Mendelssohn Performing Arts Center.)

At the time, Mom worked at Admiral. She started as a secretary, then a few months later, the company fired her boss and moved her into his position and eventually to the head of the purchasing department. That's how I got the summer job where I met Mustang David.

Mom was our personal accompanist. No matter where we sang: church, school, solo and ensemble contests, the county fair, or auditioning for a college music scholarship, Mom was always at the piano, with Dad in the audience.

I had a wonderful childhood with parents who loved me. I did what I was told without question, as did most of us who were born in the 1950s and lived in small towns. It wasn't that children were discouraged from being independent thinkers. Our TV shows like *Leave it to Beaver, Father Knows Best, The Adventures of Ozzie and Harriet,* and even *Lassie* taught us that parents knew what was best for their kids and that good behavior was a prerequisite for a happy, fulfilled life.

Choosing between my parents and Donn was the most significant decision I'd ever made up to that point. It never occurred to me until many years later that I could have chosen what was best for me.

Wedding of No Return

ON JUNE 17, 1972, NOTHING ABOUT my wedding resembled a whimsical fairy-tale celebration. Everyone looked happy enough, but no one was. Underneath those fake plastic smiles surged a wide assortment of mixed emotions.

My dad, Richard, who had accepted the engagement, wasn't happy to drive 150 miles south on Route 66 and pay for a hotel room when I could have—should have—been married in my home church, Trinity Lutheran.

My mother had resigned herself to the inevitable nuptials until my grades came in the mail a few days before the wedding, and she shouted, "You made the dean's list! Why are you throwing away a college degree, music scholarship, and a teacher's grant to marry someone thinking only of himself? If he really cared about you, he would wait until you finished college. Isn't that what you want?"

I didn't know what I wanted. The wedding plane was already in the air. I couldn't jump out now. I just wanted the wedding to be over. College funding wasn't on my radar until eight months later when the state tracked me down, and I had to repay the grant money out of my own pocket.

I didn't find out until I was writing this book that, as our wedding day drew near, Donn also felt that getting married to someone he'd only known for less than a year was a bad idea. In his words, the train had already left the station. He couldn't stop the train, and I couldn't jump out of the plane. What a pair we were!

My parents were friendly, sociable people. Even in awkward situations, they could smile as if nothing was wrong, and that's what they did when I introduced them to Donn's parents for the first time an hour before the wedding.

On the opposite side, Donn's parents were uncomfortable around people they didn't know. They barely smiled in public and *never* smiled in photos. Honestly, blank faces in every picture, like Grant Wood's painting *American Gothic* of a farmer holding a pitchfork standing next to his daughter.

Besides our fathers both working in the carpentry trade, our parents had little in common. They steered clear of each other for the rest of the day as if they had made a silent pact with their introductory handshake.

Our wedding took place at Wesley United Methodist in downtown Bloomington in a large three-story 1950s building of blonde brick. It was not Donn's home church, but he knew the minister and spent time there during his junior year at ISU when the church had a coffeehouse for college students.

Donn's home church was also named Wesley United Methodist, located in his hometown of Springfield, an hour's drive farther south on Route 66. His church was also built with blonde brick.

At first, I wondered if the monotone color scheme was required for all churches named after John Wesley, one of the Methodist movement's co-founders. As it turns out, it was typical 1950s-era architecture.

When Donn told the minister during our interview that

we wanted to get married on June 17, the minister exclaimed, "That's John Wesley's birthday!"

I thought the Wesley trio—two churches and a birthday—was just an odd coincidence. Now I think of it as foreshadowing how quickly religion would take over my life.

～ THE WEDDING ～

My white wedding dress was a simple floor-length dress with an empire waist, small collar, and small puffed sleeves, sewn from the same Simplicity Pattern as the three pink bridesmaid dresses. The material wasn't fancy. It had no sequins or train, and the shoulder-length veil didn't cover my face.

My mother wore a floor-length, sleeveless, white dress embroidered twelve inches above the hem with a lavender flower design. She wore her dark brown hair piled on top of her head in her usual upsweep style, a carryover from the late 1960s.

My red-headed father, who typically smelled of sawdust or Old Spice, wore white shoes, gray pants, and a blue sports coat with a white shirt and a navy tie. The white shoes were fashionable in the seventies, unlike his thin red beard, which covered only his jawline. I jokingly referred to it as his leprechaun disguise.

Dad's familiar cologne comforted me as we stood together next to my bridesmaids, waiting outside the sanctuary for the pipe organ to play Pachelbel's "Canon in D," indicating the processional was to begin.

Hearing our cue, the bridesmaids began their stroll down the aisle according to age, starting with the youngest, my sister Julie at thirteen, followed by Donn's sister, Susan, who was fifteen, and the maid of honor, my sister Melody, who was twenty-one.

Donn and his groomsmen, clothed in the trendy powder-blue tuxedo jacket with black lapel, black trousers, and white shoes, waited to enter the sanctuary through the side door. Hearing the music, Donn placed his hand on the doorknob, but it wouldn't open.

"A locked door? Is this an omen to not go through with the wedding?" Donn wondered.

Familiar with the church building, he placed his concern aside, walked through the sound room into the sanctuary, and opened the door for his groomsmen.

The sanctuary felt emotionally cold as I walked down the long aisle with my arm on Dad's. The blonde pews, light-colored tiled floor, blah walls, and windows thirty feet above the pews instead of at ground level made the massive sanctuary seem uninviting. Our thirty guests, who had driven many miles to attend our out-of-town wedding, appeared dwarfed at the front of the church as we walked toward them.

I should have been walking up the aisle of my home church, with its colorful stained-glass windows that entertained me when I was bored. I should have been walking on my church's red carpet, which ran from the altar area down three steps to the main floor and down the aisle. I should have been surrounded by the welcoming warmth of the beautifully carved walnut wood throughout, on the altar, the communion railings, the ceiling arches, and the hardwood floors under the pews that would have been filled with all my friends and relatives if only I'd known how to say no.

It was too late now. The wedding plane was landing. Brushing my regret aside, I kissed my dad, stood beside Donn, and focused on the only path I saw before me.

CHAPTER 5

Braceville/South Wilmington

1972 to 1973

IT WAS A BEAUTIFUL MAY EVENING a month before our wedding when we drove north on Route 66 to interview with the joint pastor-parish relations committee of the Braceville and South Wilmington Churches.

The village of Braceville, with 670 people, looked like it was in the middle of a gentle snowfall. Wisps of white from the cottonwood trees floated on the gentle spring breeze past the white church and its traditional steeple as if posing for a Christmas card.

The committee sat on one side of the room. We sat six feet away on cold metal folding chairs facing them. *Was this an interview or an interrogation?* My concern dissipated when the six members of the committee, three from each village, were friendly, asking "get to know you" questions. I spoke when spoken to, smiling the rest of the time with my teeth clenched until my jaws ached.

The interview was just a formality. Individual United Methodist churches don't hire or fire their pastors; they are appointed by the cabinet, comprised of the bishop and district superintendents.

During my years as a minister's wife, I imagined the cabinet sitting at a large table, moving clergy playing pieces around on a gameboard to make promotion runs, starting with the minister at a large church who had requested a move or was ready to retire.

For example, Pastor A is retiring. Pastor B is promoted to A's church. Pastor C is promoted to B's church. Pastor D is promoted to C's church, and so on. When the run gets to the lowest-paying church, it can go no further, and the cabinet starts another run. It isn't that simplistic, but you get the idea.

This system has advantages in that no church has to search for a minister independently. When ministers want to change jobs, they request a move and pray there is a run for them that will be a promotion, not a lateral move. It's like having access to a personal headhunter.

I think this system is pretty impressive, but it has flaws. Every promotion means a minister's family is uprooted from home and friends. And every church starts over yet again with another new minister.

Newly appointed ministers start their new job on the same Sunday, moving their families during the week prior. In 1972, the start date was the third Sunday in June, the day after my wedding, which I refer to as the no honeymoon for Gaye day.

We arrived early in South Wilmington, a village of 700 people, so Donn would have plenty of time to familiarize himself with the sanctuary and prepare for his first "official" sermon. We didn't see this church building during the interview.

The small, white, square building on the corner didn't look like a typical church. There wasn't a steeple, but it did display the United Methodist cross and red flame emblem. (This symbol was created when the Evangelical United Brethren Church and the Methodist Church merged in 1968, becoming The United Methodist Church.)

The church had two front doors on the north side of the building. We surmised that the large double door on the far left was the main entrance with stairs to the sanctuary. The smaller door on the far right appeared to lead to the basement. No one was there to greet us, so Donn parked the Opal and got out to see if the main door was open. It wasn't.

I got out of the car and stood next to him in the bright sun, wondering what was next when, without a word, he headed around the corner of the building, leaving me alone at the front door. I started around the corner to follow him, only to see his long legs turning the next corner to the back of the building. What the...?

Before he returned, a short, stocky man who had been at the interview arrived and took my hand.

"Hello, Gaye. It's good to see you again. Congratulations on the wedding! Where is the reverend?" he inquired.

Who? Oh yeah.

"He's walking around the building," I answered.

"I apologize for not being here when you arrived," he chuckled, unlocking the church door. "It didn't occur to me until a few minutes ago that you didn't yet have a key."

When Donn returned from his investigative walk, we went inside and up the steps into a foyer. As members arrived, I didn't know what was expected of me, so I stood with Donn, shaking hands, until he walked to the front of the sanctuary to sit near the podium. I found a seat in the second row.

I watched Donn calmly waiting for the organist to finish the prelude when a shadow appeared at the end of my pew, and a plump older woman glared at me. "You're in my seat," her deadpan voice announced.

I scooted five feet down the pew to give her plenty of room and, with a smile, introduced myself. "Hello, my name is Gaye. I'm married to the new minister."

She glanced in my direction, sizing me up, dismissed me with a curt, "Hello," then turned her head to the front of the church and never looked at me again.

Egads!

When the service began, Donn was introduced as the new minister, and I, the minister's wife. I would soon discover that I had officially been tossed headfirst into a boiling pot of water like an unsuspecting lobster.

It was my first day of bridehood, yet I was sitting alone in a church, downwind from a curmudgeon when I should be frolicking in bed with my new husband. What happened? Did I fall into a rabbit hole, like Alice, or was I swept into a tornado, like Dorothy? With two churches, maybe I was in both Oz and Wonderland?

But in reality, I was just a naïve eighteen-year-old who found herself in someone else's life plan. And like Alice, Dorothy, and all fairy-tale heroines, there would be a long journey of self-discovery before I found my way home.

Teenage Minister's Wife

I SAT THROUGH TWO CHURCH SERVICES that morning. Donn was an excellent speaker. There was one woman at the Braceville church who I thought was sleeping, but then I saw her jaw moving. She was a gum chewer who listened to the message with her eyes closed.

The first church was friendly, except for the "you're sitting in my seat" lady. The second church was also welcoming, but one woman had an agenda that included me. She made a bee-line to talk to me after the service.

She was an attractive brunette in her mid-forties with several booklets in her arms. She smiled as she approached, introducing herself as the Sunday school director. "Would you be willing to teach Sunday school? We could really use your help," she said with a squeaky, pleading voice.

Caught off guard, I had no idea what to say. Surely this woman could see the panic in my eyes and would lay off, but her smile and begging eyes just got bigger.

She placed her hand on her heart, leaned in closer, and with every word, nodded her head. "It's the first graders. They're a great bunch of kids. You would have a lot of fun."

I was so caught up in her Sunday school pitch that I unwittingly found myself nodding with her, which she interpreted as a yes. "That's wonderful! Thank you so much!"

Noooooo!

I was not fond of babysitting and knew nothing about teaching. That's why I was going to college. I got through high school by learning enough material to regurgitate it with moderate success. I even believed that all my friends were more intelligent than me. I squeaked by in all the heavy courses—math, science, and history—while excelling in what most people considered less important subjects—poetry, typing, shorthand, office practice, band, and choir. Even so, these courses finally got me on the honor roll in the last semester of my senior year and would eventually become the foundation for most of my adult income.

As I explained earlier, I received little information about the Bible to obtain guidance within its pages or be adept at teaching it to children. However, as a youngster, I did have a children's Bible storybook with illustrations. I specifically remember the Tower of Babel, where everyone spoke the same language until they tried to construct a tower tall enough to reach God. He shut down the project by giving them different languages so they couldn't work together.

This disturbed me. I was taught in Sunday school that God was love. If he didn't want company, why not just put a Do Not Disturb sign on a cloud or a mountain?

At home, our evening prayer was *Now I lay me down to sleep. I pray the Lord my soul to keep. If I should "sleep" before I wake, I pray the Lord my soul to take.* When I was seven, I'd lay in bed pondering, "How can I wake up if I don't sleep?"

It took several nights of contemplation before I realized that sleep was another word for death. If Mom's goal was to remove the word die so we didn't think about death right before bed, it didn't work.

In first grade, stuck in a mist tent for most of the school year due to bronchitis and tonsilitis, I would hear a high-pitched ringing in my ears. I believed it was the sound of my guardian angel working on a spinning wheel as she kept watch. I didn't see her with my eyes; it was something I sensed spiritually. You might think that congestion caused the high tone, and you're probably right; even so, it doesn't disprove that an angel was in my room.

If I did agree to teach the first grade Sunday school class, I bet the kids would believe my angel story.

I was brought out of my musing when the Sunday school director handed me the teacher and student booklets she'd been carrying. "Here you go. Thank you so much for helping."

I finally found words to respond. "But I've never taught Sunday school!"

"Oh, it's simple. Just follow the teacher's book. It tells you exactly what to do."

I read through the lesson plan for the following Sunday. She was correct; it laid out the curriculum with suggested activities and songs to complement the lesson. I might be a lousy teacher, but I knew I could play the piano and lead singing.

The Sunday school wasn't in the church building. It was in a separate, four-year-old building directly behind our house with two restrooms and five classrooms. During the week, it was used by the overcrowded public elementary school.

That following Sunday, I met my students with trepidation, expecting to relive babysitting jobs with snotty kids who wouldn't listen. I was caught off guard when they accepted me as their teacher with complete trust and fought over who would get to sit at my side.

Maybe kids aren't so bad after all?

I learned more Bible stories in two months than I remembered from my Sunday school years. During that first week, I studied the material. On Sunday, I watched their eyes light up when I read them the lesson using the stage presence I learned from acting in high school plays and singing in front of large crowds and then supplemented that information with activities and singing.

I was pretty good at this teaching gig. I even taught the older elementary students how to sing "Frère Jacques" by Jean-Philippe Rameau in rounds. (A round is when the choir sings the same melody repeatedly, but half of the group begins singing two measures after the first group starts, creating a simple harmony.)

The children sang it impressively, in French, during a church service, and no one was the wiser that it was a French nursery rhyme about a Monk who is supposed to ring the bell for prayer time but has fallen asleep.

One month into the minister's wife gig, I was invited to a United Methodist Women meeting (UMW) at the South Wilmington church. About ten women met in the basement, enjoying their coffee, tea, and cookies as they sat around two of the six heavy wooden tables that were pushed together. All the tables were homemade, painted white, and very old.

This meeting is when I realized why people expected me to do stuff. It wasn't just because I was the minister's wife. They had no idea how young I was. The only drinks this church served at meetings and potlucks were coffee, hot tea, iced tea, and tap water. I didn't drink any of that stuff. I was a kid; I drank Kool-Aid.

At the close of the meeting, the UMW president asked, "Gaye, would you close us with prayer?"

Hell no!

I ran through the only three prayers I knew, the Lord's Prayer, "Our Father, who art in heaven..." my family's meal-time prayer, "Come, Lord Jesus, be our guest..." and our confusing nighttime prayer, "If I sleep before I wake..." None of them was appropriate to close the meeting. I had no clue how to fake or improvise a prayer. They expected me to drink coffee and now pray? What was wrong with them?

With all eyes on me, I responded with a polite smile, "No, thank you."

The president smiled back. "That's fine." She saved me from humiliation by saying the prayer herself.

Sometimes the UMW would have a salad luncheon. I had no idea what that was until I attended my first one. I would have starved if there hadn't been a bowl of dinner rolls on the table. Every dish was cold: cold Jell-O salads, cold fruit salads, cold vegetable salads. My grandmother served these side dishes at Christmas and Easter. Only the adults put them on their plates.

Why would someone purposely ruin Jell-O by adding cottage cheese, shredded carrots, sliced broccoli, cauliflower, and other weird things like sunflower seeds?

Gag!

I attempted to make cherry Jell-O with fruit cocktail for my next luncheon. I poured the gelatin into a bowl, heated a cup of water to boiling, and added it to the gelatin. I stirred for the recommended two minutes, dumped in a cup of cold water and the entire can of fruit cocktail, and stirred again, transferring the concoction into a Bundt-shaped Jell-O mold I received as a wedding gift. Then I slowly walked it to the refrigerator, putting it inside to chill for four hours. When it was time to head to the luncheon, I checked the top of the Jell-O. It appeared to be firmly set.

I arrived at the luncheon early to have time to unmold the Jell-O in the kitchen. I'd seen my mother do it many times, but I'd never tried it myself. I put a large plate on top of the mold and flipped the mold and plate upside down. When I lifted the mold off the Jell-O, my potluck offering collapsed into a lumpy red wave of gelled and un-gelled fruit crashing across the countertop. Good thing it happened in the kitchen and not at the food table where the gathered women were placing their salads.

Thankfully, a woman in the kitchen rushed with me, grabbing dishtowels to stop the red sea from dripping onto the floor. Using a strainer under hot tap water, we quickly separated the fruit from the gelatin, dumping the fruit in the trash before anyone saw my mess. Then we both started to laugh.

"I feel like such an idiot! I can't even make Jell-O," I confessed.

She touched my shoulder and looked at me with a friendly chuckle. "The first time I added canned fruit to Jell-O, I didn't drain it either. The only difference between you and me is that I didn't turn it upside down."

Next time, I'll make fried egg sandwiches and serve them cold.

Cold Bedroom

NOT ONLY WERE THE LUNCHEONS COLD, but so was our bedroom, in more ways than one. Most seminary students who served the two churches lived in Chicago and only came to town on Sunday to preach, so the church parsonage had been a rental for many years. It just happened to be between renters when we moved in.

Donn and a friend with a truck had moved his belongings and furniture into the house: an itchy green sofa with a matching chair, a small television, an old kitchen table, one dresser, a twin bed, and a small desk his talented woodworking father had built in high school shop class. I have no idea how my clothing and personal belongings arrived. For all I know, a magic carpet whisked them there.

The first time I saw the inside of the parsonage was after our wedding when we stopped there to drop off wedding gifts before heading to the hotel in Kankakee for our non-honeymoon. The old, narrow, white, two-story house, most likely built in the late 1800s during the town's coal mining days, was far removed from what I envisioned.

Entering the front door, I stepped into the green-carpeted living room with dark wood paneling on the walls leading into the dining room. Off the dining room was a six-foot-by-six-foot office that housed the furnace and Donn's desk. When the paneling was installed in the house, the only cold air return was accidentally, or maybe intentionally, covered over, which meant the office/furnace room door had to always remain open during the winter months to circulate the air on the main floor. There was no air conditioning.

The dining room also led into the kitchen and bathroom, built onto what was once a narrow back porch. When the house was first built, the kitchen was in the dining room, and the outhouse was in the backyard.

Thank you for the upgrade!

As the weather turned cold, getting ready for bed became a frosty ordeal. The steep, worn wooden steps led to the second floor, which housed two bedrooms with pink and white floral wallpaper and linoleum flooring. The rooms had no closets or heat. The only spot upstairs that was warm was a two-foot-by-two-foot outcropping on the bedroom wall where the chimney ran from the furnace through our room to the roof. It was covered with the same pink floral wallpaper as the other walls. After putting my nightgown on, I would hug the chimney for five minutes to warm up before leaping under the chilly sheets. If I could have figured out how to strap myself to that chimney, I would have slept standing up.

On our second day at the house, we drove to Sears to buy two cheap portable closets, a dresser, a chest, two nightstands, and a queen-size bed.

After church on the second Sunday, Donn packed up the Opal station wagon and headed out of town for a week to do his high school church camp counselor thing. I understood this was something he did every summer. Still, I wasn't happy about being left alone without a vehicle in a town without friends or a grocery store.

The silence in the house was deafening. Although I enjoyed being alone while living at my parents' house, there was always the reassurance that someone would eventually come home. Even at college when my roommate was out of town, people were always within earshot. At least I had one thing to look forward to. My uncle and aunt from Florida, whom I hadn't seen in five years, would stop by the next day on their way home from visiting family in Harvard.

When Donn arrived at the campgrounds, Dave, the camp director, discovered Donn had left his new bride at home. Dave insisted that Donn drive the two and a half hours back to Braceville to bring me to camp to serve as a counselor.

Donn called me mid-afternoon, apologizing for not checking if I could also have attended. "I will drive back to get you if you want to come."

Yes!

And then, I had an idea. "I might be able to get a ride there. Stay close to the payphone. I'll call you right back."

The following day, my relatives and I visited in the car as they drove 140 miles out of their way to drop me off at camp. Leaving the paved road at the Epworth Springs United Methodist Camp sign, we headed down a long gravel road sandwiched between two cornfields and an old cemetery on our left.

Making a hard left turn at a farmhouse and a right turn along a row of tall trees, we came upon a slew of cabins and a swimming pool. With wet hair from their recent swim, elementary school kids blocked the road as they headed to the dining hall for lunch.

I attended a Lutheran church camp once when I was ten. I despised stumbling outside at night with a flashlight to get to the bathhouse and being forced to sit alone under a tree every morning to read the boring Bible. Lucky for me, during this Methodist camping experience, the high school campers and staff would sleep inside the bunkhouse in the same building as the dining hall. Girls in one large room, boys in the other.

The high schoolers accepted me as a counselor even though I was more of a chaperone. Like the church members, the campers thought I was much older. My actual age was an advantage in connecting with the female campers. I could sincerely empathize when they talked about their parents not liking their boyfriend and how disappointed they were that they weren't asked to prom. I must have been doing something right because during the week, I was told many times, "You're a great listener!"

Donn added all the energy to the camp experience. At least I wasn't a tag-along this time. However, Donn and I spent no time alone. We rarely talked or sat together for meals because we had to sit with our group of kids. At least I wasn't sitting alone at home.

Back in Braceville, word got around that Donn had a music degree, and the local high school offered him a part-time position teaching choir after school. He was in his element, teaching music and pastoring the churches. His two loves, together at last.

What wasn't working for him were the classes he was taking at the junior college. They were geared toward first-year college students, not college graduates. He dropped out after two weeks and registered for the spring semester with different instructors.

Donn dedicated all his energy to creating memorable experiences and activities for those he served, not just the music students and the youth in the church but activities for the adults as well, like monthly hymn sing-alongs, walkathons to raise money for charity, and gathering clothing for a family in need.

Donn's commitment to God was impressive as he focused on serving others. I would catch glimpses of him checking his pocket watch as he ran out the door with those long, fast-moving legs to minister to his congregations.

As for me, I missed my family and friends. The loneliness was sometimes gut-wrenching. I felt lost and unloved. How does one compete with God?

I went to bed at night, hoping that when the sun rose in the morning, I would wake up in my warm bed at my parents' house and discover that my life was just a bad dream. Unfortunately, that didn't happen.

Feeling responsible for bringing money into the household, I got a job in a factory nine miles away in Mazon, a small farming community. I carpooled with two women, best friends, whose children were married to each other. We got along fine but had little in common. Even their children were older than me.

When it comes to finances, I've always been a saver. I once overheard my mother joking with her friend that I stuffed my mattress with dollar bills. Not true! I stored money in a bank account like everyone else. Dimes, however, were saved in glass cigar tubes in my dresser drawer. Dad got them from a friend and gave them to me to save dimes.

Every week in high school, I received five dollars for school lunches. The spare change was mine to use however I wanted: school supplies, personal items, etc. When I received the glass tubes, I started eating school lunches four days a week instead of five because I got two dollars back and one dime to put into the cigar tube.

The factory in Mazon, called Assemblies or Kords, was in an old building half the size of a basketball court. For $1.60 an hour, the minimum wage back then, I sat at a machine that looked similar to a sewing machine, but it put terminals on the ends of wires.

My carpool ladies and ten other women also sat at one. The thump, thump, thump of machines at various speeds bounced off the concrete floors and walls with a collision of noise. We should have been wearing earplugs. Although the Occupational Safety and Health Administration was created in 1970, they didn't require earplugs to protect workers in noisy environments until 1981.

As I sat in the clatter, placing the end of a wire into my machine and tapping a pedal with my foot to attach the terminal to the wire, I turned the work into a game to pass the time, challenging myself to go faster and faster.

I was a speedy, efficient worker, which the boss appreciated. A few months later, I received a ten-cent raise and was moved to a tall, specialized machine where I sat on a comfortable barstool with my feet off the floor. It was the best seat in the house when the field mice came inside in September to scamper through the building during the harvest season.

This new machine put rubber coating around the terminals made by the other female workers. I poured small black rubber pellets into a chute to be melted. Then I attached one of the wired terminals to the machine. When I tapped the foot pedal, the terminal went into the machine and came out with rubber surrounding it.

Voilà!

Factory work was supposed to be just a high school summer job. I was good at manual labor, but it wasn't what I wanted to do with my life.

When I was sixteen, I worked with a partner in a laundry folding hot sheets as they came off a mangle, searing my fingers while sweat dripped from my armpits into my shoes. (A mangle is a massive machine with hot rollers that press large pieces of cloth.)

When working at Admiral Corporation for the next two summers soldering wires, my coworkers showed me how to protect my fingers with masking tape.

My dream was to teach music, yet here I was in another factory while Donn was living his dream. The Pollyanna in me looked for the silver lining, but even she couldn't find it. Cut off from family and friends, I was too old to hang out with the teenagers in our church and too young to hang out with their parents. I didn't fit in anywhere.

I wasn't the minister, but neither was I a typical parishioner; I was a bonus gift that came with the purchase of a pastor. I was a doodad you don't take out of the box, like my unopened *Star Trek: The Next Generation* twenty-five-year anniversary Pez Dispenser Collector Series that sits next to my Mr. Spock Christmas ornament on the shelf behind me as I write.

No one my age attended our churches. Even if they did, I couldn't tell a parishioner I felt invisible in my marriage. So, wearing a plastic smile, I pretended everything was okay in front of the church members, coworkers, and even my husband.

Rather than wallowing in my current situation, I looked at my finances. I still had money from summer jobs in high school, so I registered for the spring semester at Joliet Junior College and found a local JJC student happy to have someone to talk to on the thirty-five-minute drive to school. Then I called my mother, apologized for not listening to her, and told her I was going back to college at the end of January.

In December, I left the factory for a temporary two-month evening shift job at R&R Donnelly, making $2.90 an hour collating telephone books. I carpooled with a part-time police-man from our town who also worked there.

My workplace was on a dock with twenty-five other men and women. We stood above the assembly line machine that collated each phone book section, loading them into their respective chutes, where they quickly dropped down to merge on the assembly line. Because I was so busy hauling armfuls of my sections from the stacks behind me and carefully placing them into their chute, there was no time to take a break to use the restroom. I had to get the attention of the roaming substi-tute to put me on the bathroom list, then wait for my turn to pee.

Even though I wore an apron, my hands and arms were so filthy from the ink on the paper that when I returned home at 11 p.m., I took a shower before hugging the chimney and get-ting into bed.

During those two months, we made our weekly quota once. Our supervisor proudly handed each of us a shiny fifty-cent piece for all our hard work. *Are you kidding me?* I didn't com-plain. The job was nearly over and paid almost double what I made at my last job.

On January 22, all machines suddenly stopped. Over the factory intercom, we were told that Lyndon B. Johnson, U.S. president from 1963 to 1969, had died of a heart attack.

On January 29, I was a college student again with seven classes: history, rhetoric, and five music classes. Donn was also a student but dropped out again a few weeks later.

When I discovered Donn had scheduled a youth trip to Gatlinburg, Tennessee, on the same day of my band and choir concert, which I had to attend to get a passing grade, I was right back where I was the year before, choosing between my college degree and Donn.

I was the only bass clarinet in the band and had a solo in the choir. How could I let my fellow musicians down? But I did. To avoid two failing grades, I dropped both band and choir. Yet, another college derailment, but I did earn fourteen more credit hours toward my degree.

Our three-car caravan, two driven by parents and one by us, took the teens (technically, I was still a teen at nineteen) to the Smoky Mountains. The flowing rivers gurgling along the roadways and the beautifully magnificent trees that hid houses from our view filled me with awe. Spending time in nature was worth losing those college credits.

Eat, Pray, Puke

THE 1960S HIPPY MOVEMENT WAS A counterculture of young middle-class Americans who challenged society's values. They were rebellious activists advocating individuality, peace, love, drugs, communal living, anti-war, anti-government, and anti-materialism.

Many of these long-haired hippies saw Jesus as a like-minded rabble-rouser who also lived a minimalist lifestyle, traveled the countryside with his pals, and challenged the political and religious status quo. Jesus became their hero and inspiration to bring excitement and inspiration back into mainstream Christianity.

They held rallies to encourage the thousands of drug-addicted hippies in Haight-Ashbury to save themselves by following Jesus, the peaceful agitator who opened the minds of the masses two thousand years earlier. (Haight-Ashbury is a district of San Francisco where the hippy movement began.) As more and more hippies turned to Jesus, the 1970s Jesus movement was born, spreading like wildfire across the USA.

I had never heard of the Jesus movement until one of our church members told us they owned a two-story farmhouse in the country that they rented to a Jesus commune. Curious, I went with Donn on a bright sunny day to meet this hippie group that lived together.

The friendly tenants were laid back, calm, quiet, and easy to talk to. What I remember most about them was their constant, "Thank you, Jesus." It was a tagline on every sentence. "We grow our own vegetables. Thank you, Jesus." "It was so nice of you to stop by for a visit. Thank you, Jesus." I thought the thank-yous were a bit over the top, but what did I know? Maybe it was a commune rule.

Although Donn didn't use their commune tagline, he also had a lot of enthusiasm for Jesus, which the older seasoned Methodist ministers didn't appreciate. They probably would have found our wall posters irreverent.

One poster was of an older, bald, white male preaching in a black robe from a church pulpit. A long-haired, bearded Jesus wearing a white robe and sandals is asleep on the front pew with his head on the shoulder of the person on his left. His legs are crossed. His right arm rests on the back of the pew, and his left is on his lap.

I thought the image was hilarious! I'd sat through plenty of dull sermons in the Lutheran church to identify with a bored, sleeping Jesus.

The second poster still makes me giggle. It looked like a child's drawing of God, with a carrot-like nose, a crown on his head, and an arm up in the air announcing, in a child's handwriting, *Earth, this is God! I want all you people to clear out before the end of the month. I have a client who's interested in the property.*

The last poster was in the form of a wanted poster.

WANTED: JESUS CHRIST
Alias: *The Messiah, The Son of God, King of Kings,
Lord of Lords, Prince of Peace, etc.*
Notorious leader of an underground liberation movement. Wanted for the following charges: practicing medicine, winemaking, and food distribution without a license.

Interfering with businessmen in the temple. Associating with known criminals, radicals, subversives, prostitutes, and street people. Claiming to have the authority to make people into God's children.
APPEARANCE: *Typical hippie type—long hair, beard, robe, sandals. Hangs around slum areas, few rich friends, often sneaks out into the desert.*
BEWARE: *This man is extremely dangerous. His insidiously inflammatory message is particularly dangerous to young people who haven't been taught to ignore him yet. He changes men and claims to set them free.*
WARNING: HE IS STILL AT LARGE!

Although I grew up in the church, I didn't know who Jesus was other than what the creeds told me: born, crucified, died, buried, rose from the dead, walked on water, and turned water into wine. These accomplishments revealed nothing about his character. It wasn't until I saw these posters that I began to think of Jesus in a different light: a hippie with an attitude who sleeps during church, a notorious leader who challenges the status quo, and someone who would laugh with me at a poster of God kicking us off the planet. I really liked this guy!

Donn put together a Jesus rally at the park in South Wilmington with help from the commune and one of our church members, who brought in a flatbed trailer to use as a stage. Everyone in the area was invited to bring their chairs and blankets, sit in the sunshine, hear the Jesus People preach about Jesus, and enjoy their modern uplifting music. I liked this toe-tapping, easy-to-sing Christian music with guitars and drums. The event was like a tiny version of Woodstock without sex and drugs.

I spent the day in the audience sitting alone on a blanket behind the teens and in front of the adults who sat on lawn chairs. Donn was busy on stage introducing singing groups and speakers. He was in his happy space, the excitement visible on his face.

Near the end of the rally, the Jesus People invited the audience to the stage. "We've all sinned and fallen short of the glory of God. If you want joy in your life, come up and be saved. Give your life to Jesus, cleanse your soul, and be born again!"

My Lutheran church never preached that we were sinners or had to accept Jesus as our savior to get to heaven, but I yearned for joy. My name, Gaye, means merry and happy. My mother wrote in my baby book, "Gaye is always smiling and happy to have anyone talk to her." But I wasn't happy anymore, at least not deep down inside. I knew my alter ego, Pollyanna, was on her deathbed, slowly slipping away, but I didn't know how to save her.

My heart pounded when the youth from our two churches headed to the stage. I wanted to join them, save Pollyanna, and feel normal again, but my legs wouldn't move. And then there was the big concern: What would the congregation think if their minister's wife went forward?

Through the Jesus commune, Donn was introduced to Paul, who invited us to Chicago to attend a Friday evening charismatic prayer meeting. I had no idea what to expect.

People get together on date night to pray?

Donn and I drove seventy-five miles to Paul's apartment on North Lake Shore Drive overlooking Lake Michigan. Before the prayer meeting, he took us to dinner at a Chinese restaurant. I'd never had authentic Chinese food before. Donn hadn't either. I studied the menu with no clue about what was in the dishes. Who was General Tso? Was Mongolian beef actually from Mongolia? Is Kung Pao a place or a person? Where was the American chop suey that my mother made from a can?

Noticing my indecision, Paul suggested a dish that I then ordered. I was not fond of it, but I ate it to be polite. After dinner, my head started hurting as Paul drove us to the prayer meeting at a small chapel with about fifty people in attendance. The event seemed normal until the entire group began to pray out loud, not in unison like a responsive reading, but everyone vocalizing their own prayers loudly—at the same time.

The more they prayed, the louder they got, as if God was hard of hearing. After a few minutes, their words faded into gibberish. I'd heard of speaking in tongues but had never seen it in action. Then the room got hot, my head started pounding, and I felt nauseous. I left the chapel, stepped into the cool hallway to fan my face, and waited for the date night prayer thing to end.

My symptoms worsened when I rode in the back seat of Paul's little sports car on the way to his place. *Hurry up, Paul. Hurry up!*

When he parked, I bolted out of the car and puked all that Chinese food into the bushes by the front door. I was embarrassed but feeling much better; the headache simmered to a mild ache around the eyes and neck.

Paul's female friend Jean, who had met us at the prayer meeting, joined us in his apartment after witnessing my impromptu shrubbery fertilization.

"I bet you're allergic to the MSG in Chinese food," she said.

MSG? Never heard of it.

"Sit in this chair, and I'll massage your neck."

Ah! Her hands were soothing. With each movement on my

neck, the ache released its hold. I'd never heard of massage for headaches. I'd never heard of massage, period! But since that day, I've avidly supported its ability to relieve tension and pain.

After that trip, we had several more adventures in the Windy City. We saw *Jesus Christ Super Star* and *Hair* on stage. The theater lights were turned down too low during the naked scene in *Hair* to see any body parts. I also went to my first *Ice Capades* show when I was invited to be a chaperone for the local Girl Scout troop's trip to Chicago.

I gathered a lot of worldly experiences in religion, food, theater, and entertainment the first year we were married.

CHAPTER 9

Friend Request

DONN WAS GOOD AT HIS JOB, going above and beyond his Sunday responsibilities. I admired his creative ability to think outside the box, but that didn't change my feelings about being his shadow.

He had lived alone for two years making all his own decisions. I had never lived alone. If we had dated longer, we would've known more about each other's likes and dislikes. During the first week of our marriage, Donn made breakfast. As I entered the kitchen, I caught him doing the unthinkable and screamed, "Why are you putting ketchup on my scrambled eggs?"

On New Year's Day, he said, "Let's go to a movie."

"Sure, what's playing?"

"It's a surprise," he replied.

"I don't like surprises. What are we seeing?" I asked again as we headed to Joliet.

"I'm positive you'll like it; trust me."

Like everything else lately, it was my first time in a multiplex movie theater. Donn bought tickets for *The Poseidon Adventure*, one of the first disaster movies made in the 1970s. This one was about a cruise ship on New Year's Eve with fourteen hundred people on board that capsized when it was hit broadside by a tsunami.

Within the first thirty minutes, the all-star cast was down to about twenty survivors. I watched with clenched teeth and a thumping heart as they worked their way through the upside-down ship, deck by deck, trying to escape the rising water rushing up from below them in their attempt to make it to the bottom of the ocean liner, which was now above them. Only a handful escaped through a hole cut into the hull by a rescue team.

I couldn't speak at all on the drive home. I was too busy choking back tears. It says a lot about a marriage when you don't want your spouse to see you cry. We didn't know the first thing about making a marriage work. We weren't a team collaborating on a project. We lived together, but we were apart. We were two kids playing house who barely knew each other, pretending to be a couple. With the added responsibility of two churches, we had little time to get to know ourselves, let alone each other.

On April 20, 1973, Donn held an afternoon Good Friday service, a solemn commemoration of the day Jesus was crucified on the cross. I felt down that day, having just dropped the two college classes. The first somber death hymn, "Were You There When They Crucified My Lord," didn't help my mood.

For the past nine months, I'd been mourning the loss of my childhood—a time when I never questioned if I was loved. We'd been to several Jesus rallies with fervent speakers who asserted that I would be miraculously happy if I gave my life to Jesus. Still, I never went to the stage, even though I desperately wanted to feel joy again.

I stood with the congregation for the second hymn, "What a Friend We Have in Jesus," but I couldn't sing with the massive lump in my throat. Tears welled up, and then Loneliness spoke to me. "You've been carrying this sorrow inside of you for too long. It's time to let it go."

I know.

"You need a friend."

Yes, I do.

"You need a friend who will never leave you."

And then I heard the song's lyrics, "Can we find a friend so faithful who will all our sorrow share? Jesus knows our every weakness. Take it to the Lord in prayer."

Keeping my eyes focused on the floor so no one could see my wet face, I quietly slipped down the church aisle and out the door. Rushing around the corner of the church to the house, I knelt in front of the scratchy green sofa and wept.

I didn't confess that I was a sinner. I didn't ask to be cleansed, saved, or born again. I didn't say anything; I didn't think I had to. The bucket of salty tears and snot on the sofa was all I needed to send a friend request to the spirit world.

When my anguished sobs eased, I lifted my head with a calm sense of peace in that I was safe. Not saved, but safe. How could I be saved from God's wrath while at the same time believing God is love?

Positive Pollyanna was back, her crutches tossed aside, walking tall, and we didn't have to go forward to an altar or a flatbed trailer to make it happen. In the words of the Jesus People, I was born again—a new me to look at the world with fresh eyes, knowing that I was not alone. The spirit world was on my side.

I want to say that this book isn't a marketing tool for God, Jesus, or any one faith. It's a journey of self-discovery that begins in religion but expands into something much bigger.

I was so excited about my newfound spiritual life that I dove into the New Testament my dad gave me as if I were one of Acapulco's famous cliff divers. I carried it to college and read it during lunch, and in bed after hugging the chimney for warmth.

When we visited my parents a few weeks later, I couldn't wait to tell them how happy I was in this new relationship with the spirit world. I remember standing in the kitchen, going on and on about my exciting relationship with Jesus and how it changed my life.

"Gaye, I'd like to talk with you in the living room," Mom said as she headed out of the kitchen.

Uh oh. What did I do now?

"I get the feeling that you think I'm not a Christian, and I'm very hurt," she said with tears glistening.

"I'm so sorry, Mom. That's not what I think," I lied.

Mom was right. I had assumed she wasn't a Christian because I believed all Christians were supposed to be super excited, like the Jesus People. But mostly, I just wanted to share with my mom what gave me joy.

We hugged, and all seemed to be okay, but I was racked with guilt that I had hurt her again. I learned an excellent lesson. Each person is unique, and we will never fully understand who someone else is on the inside. It's none of our business anyway.

Once, I overheard Mom say, "Don't talk about religion or politics; it just causes problems." So out of fear of hurting people I loved, I stopped talking about my spirituality in front of them, choosing instead to hide the most significant aspect of my life, with music now coming in second.

Kentucky
1975 to 1976

WHEN DONN DROPPED THOSE CLASSES AT Joliet Junior, he was still a licensed lay minister. However, we had to leave because he hadn't fulfilled the student pastor requirement to attend classes. We packed our belongings and moved to Springfield.

We had several jobs in the two years we lived in the area. Donn built inground swimming pools and worked at a shoe store. I was a clerk typist at the Illinois Department of Public Aid, a secretary at the Illinois Country Opry, and I gave private voice lessons.

We started a music ministry singing gospel and upbeat Jesus People songs and recorded two vinyl albums we sold at our gigs. Thirty years later, at a book sale, I thumbed through a box of old albums, finding John Denver, The Monkeys, and Herb Alpert & the Tijuana Brass, and said, "Wouldn't it be something if I found one of my albums?"

And there it was, the first one we recorded in 1973, *To the Glory of God*. I bought it for fifty cents. A few years later, the second album, *Gifts*, recorded in 1975, showed up on eBay for an opening bid of $6.95. My face was a bit fuller on the back cover—I was pregnant with our first child.

Music was the one thing we both had in common. I sang the melody while Donn sang a tight harmony below me. On the weekends, we traveled to churches throughout central

Illinois, performing concerts on Saturday evenings or during the Sunday service, sometimes both. Donn was an exceptional musician accomplished on the trumpet, accordion, and piano. More than once, the ivories on old church upright pianos would fly off as he played.

I was comfortable talking to people and singing in front of a large crowd, but I wanted nothing to do with public speaking. So, Donn introduced all the songs from the piano while I stood quietly near him, waiting for my cue to start singing.

The interesting thing about spiritual songs is that I feel very close to the spirit world when I sing. Once, after singing a solo, a woman named Ruth pulled me into a gentle hug and whispered, "When you open your mouth, God falls out."

In May 1975, we moved from Illinois into a two-bedroom duplex in Nicholasville, Kentucky, so Donn could start the summer semester at Asbury Theological Seminary in Wilmore. The town and seminary are known for the Ichthus Music Festival, a Christian response to Woodstock. This annual event began in the spring of 1970 at the beginning of the Jesus Movement.

I was now seven months pregnant and 450 miles away from my family, spending my time setting up housekeeping and watching TV, specifically *Ryan's Hope*, a soap opera launched that summer starring Kate Mulgrew as Mary Ryan. (Kate went on to portray Captain Katherine Janeway in *Star Trek: Voyager*, one of my favorite *Star Trek* TV shows.)

My mother called weekly to tell me what was happening at home and check in on me.

"Hi, sweetheart. How are you feeling today?"

"Other than swollen ankles, I'm fine. I've been craving French toast. Is that weird?"

"No, that's not weird."

"We're having problems with our car. It's been in the shop two times already." I didn't tell her that our health insurance covered me but not the baby or that the car repairs were depleting the money we had saved for the hospital bill.

"Oh my! I hope your car gets fixed before the baby comes. Are you eating enough? Are you happy?"

"Yes, and yes. I have a new friend, Dee. Her husband is the Methodist minister in town. She's pregnant with their second child and due around the same time. The four of us are taking Lamaze classes to learn how to use breathing techniques to relax during childbirth."

Mom chuckled. "When I was pregnant, they just knocked me out, and when I woke up, you were there."

At six-thirty in the morning on August 8, when I was twenty-two years old, my water broke. Unfortunately, our car was in the shop for the fourth time. We traded the lemon a month later for a used Dodge Dart.

Donn called Howard, Dee's husband, who drove us to Central Baptist Hospital. The men casually chatted about church stuff in the front seat as if it was an ordinary day while I sat on two towels in the back seat, leaking fluid with every contraction.

Thankfully, Howard looked in his rearview mirror, noticed the grimace on my face, and, with his calm voice, transformed into a Lamaze coach. "Find a focal point in front of you, Gaye, and take a deep breath in through your nose, and slowly let it out. In...and out."

Thank you, Howard!

Donn walked me into the emergency room as amniotic fluid dripped down my legs, leaving a long trail on the floor as if a giant slug had just wandered through the door. Five and a half hours later, the nurse placed Michael in my arms. My first thought was, *He's beautiful.* The second was, *They taught me how to get him here, but they didn't teach me what to do with him once I got him. Oh well, I'll figure it out.*

The hospital expected full payment before I could leave, but our savings were now gone. I don't remember how much the bill was, but it was minuscule compared to today's hospital prices. Howard and Dee kindly covered the cost with the request that we pay it forward. Their little boy arrived the following week.

Mom flew in for five days to help me acclimate to motherhood and nursing. After dropping her off at the airport and watching her plane take to the sky, I cried all the way home.

Michael slept most of the time that Mom was with us, then right after she left, he woke up, taking just one nap in the morning and one in the afternoon and crying every evening from six to ten.

My attempts to calm him down were exhausting. Desperate, I defied the advice of my nursing support group and stopped feeding him every time he cried. I put him in his crib at eight o'clock in the evening and let him cry himself to sleep. It wasn't easy to listen to those screams and not go to him. Within three days, he was no longer crying in the evening and went to sleep as soon as I laid him down.

Donn attended seminary in the morning, taught music every afternoon at a public school forty miles away, and then studied at home after dinner. I couldn't complain about his unavailability since he was the only one putting food on the table. However, when I dragged my exhausted body out of bed at three o'clock in the morning to nurse our crying child, the fact that Donn got to sleep through the night pissed me off. According to the nursing support group, a mother should never feed her child when angry; it could harm the baby's health. I ignored that advice too.

To counter the dark night feelings, I wrote positive affirmations on poster boards with colorful magic markers and plastered them all over the kitchen walls. I remember *Bloom Where You Are Planted*, *When Life Gives You Lemons, Make Lemonade*, and *Today Is the First Day of the Rest of Your Life*.

One day, I said, "Now that I have a child, I'm gonna need a sewing machine." When I opened the front door the following morning to let in the sunshine, a sewing machine was on the front porch that we shared with our duplex neighbor. She was having a yard sale. I bought her mother's old machine for five dollars. It wasn't the best, but it did what I needed.

All I said was, "I'm gonna need a sewing machine," and there it was. I didn't realize it then, but this wasn't the first time I manifested things. Jobs were handed to me when I needed money, and carpoolers showed up when I needed a ride for employment and college. Little did I know then that manifesting would be a reoccurring part of my life. Even in high school, I had a friend who said, "Gaye, you could fall into a mud puddle and still come out smelling like a rose."

I enjoyed being a mother once Michael began sleeping through the night, but I was getting a little stir-crazy being in the house all day. I wasn't an avid reader but needed something to do, so I asked Donn to bring me a book from the seminary library. The librarian recommended *The Lion, the Witch, and the Wardrobe*, the first book written in the *Chronicles of Narnia* by C. S. Lewis. I read only when Michael was napping. Since he didn't sleep long, I read as fast as possible, zipping through the pages. It's incredible how a naptime incentive can turn a person into a speed reader.

I joined a Christian women's book club. We studied *You Can Be the Wife of a Happy Husband: Discovering the Keys to Marital Success* by Darian B. Cooper. It taught that the woman is responsible for making her husband and children happy because being a homemaker is the Christian wife's role.

I also read *The Total Woman: How to Make Your Marriage Come Alive!* by Marabel Morgan, a book on saving your marriage by being a submissive Christian wife. I was to pamper my husband, walk him to the car in the morning, soothe all his frustrations with sex, and greet him at the door wearing a sexy outfit. I heard of a woman who, after reading this book, greeted her husband at the door in nothing but Saran Wrap. I am mortified to admit that I bought into some of this nonsense.

Donn offered to watch Michael on Saturdays so I could get out of the house, but there was no place to go or extra money to spend. What I wanted was time alone in the house. Unfortunately, that wish wouldn't come true for another fourteen years.

In January of 1976, when Michael was six months old, my parents drove from Illinois to Kentucky to help us move to a small town of a thousand people where Donn was teaching band, choir, and music theory. I hid my tears when they left, just like in October when they drove home after Michael's baptism.

We moved because Donn needed to be at the school in the evenings to direct the basketball pep band and the spring musical, *H. M. S. Pinafore*. It had been many years since the school had these activities. I was proud of my husband for giving his students these extra special memories, but he was gone more now than before.

One advantage of the move was that I had access to our car in the afternoon when Donn was teaching. Once a week,

I would take Michael with me to get groceries and check out books at the library seven miles away in a town of sixty-seven hundred. I would sing to him in the car both there and back. "Itsy Bitsy Spider" was his favorite.

This town also had a large Methodist church. Instead of choir practice on a weekday evening, it was on Sunday before church, and they had a nursery for Michael when we rehearsed. I was thrilled to sing in a choir again. I missed singing with Dee at the Nicholasville church, where we sat next to each other in the choir loft, trying to figure out which one of us was being summoned by the frantically waving nursery helper at the back of the church.

The old house we rented near the school belonged to a woman and her elderly mother. The main floor had a bedroom for Michael and a spacious living room with a wide archway into the large dining room, where we slept. The small kitchen sported a five-foot-wide antique white cast-iron single sink with a drainboard. One wall held a few small plywood cupboards.

The landlady and her mother lived in a new house they had just built next to ours. Both homes were on their water bill. When we moved in, the mother said she only flushed her toilet once daily and asked us to do the same.

You've got to be kidding me!

Pampers disposable diapers were invented in 1961, but I used them sparingly only for church and travel. Every mother I knew still used cloth diapers for home use. We all rinsed poopy diapers in the toilet by holding onto one corner and holding it tight when we flushed.

At least one diaper, maybe two, slipped from my fingers and disappeared during my childrearing years. The rinsed diapers that didn't end up in the sewer went into a diaper pail. It was absurd to ask a family, especially one with a baby, to flush the toilet only once a day. I did not comply with the old lady's wishes.

Alone most of the time, with only Michael for company, I lived for Mom's weekly phone call. On one of those calls, Mom said Michael and I could move in with her and Dad. It took me days to get up enough courage to tell Donn the news. I waited until we were in bed before I told him, "I want Michael and me to move in with my parents. Will you take us to the airport?"

I lay in bed, barely breathing, waiting for a response. Eventually, he quietly whispered, "I don't want to lose my family."

It was naïve of me to think he would agree to my plan. I considered sneaking out of town with the car when he was teaching school, but all the books said my job as a Christian wife was to ensure my husband's happiness. What would God think if I left my spouse stranded without a vehicle?

We couldn't afford another semester of seminary, and the part-time music position didn't pay over the summer. Donn contacted the conference office, inquiring about open church-related positions back home. In June, we headed back to Illinois.

Mattoon

1976 to 1978

DONN WAS HIRED AS THE DIRECTOR of Christian Education at a large United Methodist Church in east central Illinois in a town of 19,700 people. We moved into the associate minister's house, a beautiful modern two-story with four bedrooms, two baths, a finished basement, a backyard with grapevines, and a two-car garage. It had heat in every room. I was happy.

Vivian, the seasoned wife of the head minister, took me under her wing. I listened to her advice as if it came directly from the angel Gabriel. In November, she pulled me aside after church. "I'm having an open house the second Sunday in December. Have you considered having one in the associate parsonage?"

Her suggestion caught me off guard. I thought only people celebrating their fiftieth wedding anniversaries had open houses.

"Why would I have an open house?"

"Members enjoy seeing their parsonages at Christmas time. I'm sure they will be disappointed if they don't see yours. I have one every Christmas. It's good for public relations if you know what I mean," she added, lightly punching my arm.

Donn had already planned an overnight fun and games retreat for the youth in our basement the night before the date of Vivian's open house. I didn't share this info with her, fearing it might jeopardize Donn's job. I liked our new home and wanted to live in it for a long time.

"I suppose I could have one the Sunday before or after yours."

"Oh goodness no, dear. The church members prefer to go to both houses on the same day."

"Oh, Okay."

"Great!" Vivian then began counting on her fingers as she talked. "You will need cookies. I'll arrange for the United Methodist Women to make them for you. You'll need coffee, tea, punch, a punch bowl, dishes, cups, festive napkins, and some women to fill the cookie trays and wash dishes."

Dishes? I envisioned a pitcher of Kool-Aid and a Tupperware container of cookies on the kitchen counter. The church had stacks of white napkins, Styrofoam cups, and paper plates I could use. I completely disregarded her list.

Vivian had already turned to leave, then hesitated, turned back around, and said, "It would be a good idea to hire someone to keep Michael out of the way. Little children can be a nuisance when the house is filled with people." Then she left.

I stood with my mouth open as my squinty eyes tossed knives at her back. How dare she tell me to keep my child out of the way! My opinion of her came crashing down. I didn't care what she thought of me. I was doing my open house with Styrofoam, paper, and my toddler.

Two weeks before the event, Vivian stopped by our house to give me a punch recipe and loan me a coffee maker from the church kitchen. And then, another woman from church stopped by with an early Christmas gift—a brand-new punch bowl, even though I already had one. I sensed a conspiracy, so I kept my mouth shut.

Vivian called me periodically. "Have you found some ladies to help you in the kitchen?"

"I don't need anyone," I countered.

"You need help, Gaye. You get on the phone right now and make some calls."

OOH! That woman irritated me. How dare she tell me what to do.

The Monday before the open house, Vivian called again. "I just heard Donn scheduled an all-night party at your house Saturday night. What is he trying to prove? If I were you, I'd tell him to call it off. There is plenty of time for the church secretary to call all the teens' parents and cancel the party."

I knew that would be her reaction. I had reservations about the overnight too. I pictured a nuclear missile testing site the morning after the party that I would be cleaning up, but I wasn't about to confess that to Vivian. I was determined to have that party in my house even if I had to drag the kids to it myself.

I tried to sound unconcerned. "I'm not the least bit worried, Vivian."

"You're not?"

"Nope."

"Well, it's your house."

It damn well is!

I told Donn about Vivian's call when he came home for lunch. "Would you please ensure the house is in perfect order Sunday morning when the kids leave?"

"You won't have to do a thing," he promised.

The overnight went well, but I didn't stay up for all the festivities. I awoke on Sunday morning to the sound of the vacuum cleaner and the smell of Pledge furniture polish. I didn't have to lift a finger. The kids did all the work.

After the worship service, Vivian stopped me in the church parlor, asking about the overnight.

"No problem!" I boasted. "The house looks great."

And then Vivian asked, "Did you ever find someone to help you in the kitchen?"

Why won't she let it go?

"No, I didn't." I was getting ready to add, "I don't need help," when Vivian stopped June and Pat as they walked by.

"Gaye needs help in the kitchen this afternoon for her open house. Would you be available to help her?"

"We'd be delighted," they responded. "What time should we be there?"

Before I could answer, Vivian replied, "One-thirty." Then she turned to face me. "Do you need more trays for the cookies?"

June popped in with, "Oh, I have lots of trays."

"So do I," added Pat. We'll bring them with us. See you at one-thirty, Gaye."

Vivian ended the conversation with, "Well, now, I think we have everything ready for you." I stood, dazed, as the three women rushed off to their Sunday school class.

What just happened? Was this another setup? Steam shot out of my ears. I wanted to scream aloud, "It's not your party, VIVIAN!" But why bother? No matter how assertive I tried to be, this woman always got what she wanted.

June and Pat promptly showed up at one-thirty. They started the coffee (no tea), put the punch ingredients I'd bought into my new punch bowl, and arranged the UMW-baked cookies on their festive trays. They thought my white napkins and paper cups were fine. They also agreed that my invitees could help themselves.

The ladies kept the cookie trays and punch bowl filled, so

all I had to do was visit with my guests. I appreciated their help and support of me and decided to believe they weren't in on Vivian's manipulation.

Vivian and I avoided each other as much as we could after that. The following December, she scheduled her yearly open house. I'd recently had a miscarriage, which got me out of having guests at my house. However, I did attend her party. Children weren't allowed, so Donn stayed home with Michael.

During the three-hour open house, Vivian had six women lined up to help during each hour. Two women stood at the linen-covered refreshment table pouring coffee and tea from a silver service, two washed glass cups and plates in the kitchen, and another two kept the cookie trays filled. I spoke to the women in charge of the kitchen and discovered that Vivian had been baking and freezing cookies for the past three months.

I watched Vivian's guests sitting stiff and uncomfortable, quietly conversing while balancing china plates and cups on their laps. A year earlier, at my house, they were laughing, using paper plates and Styrofoam cups, and playing on the floor with Michael.

It occurred to me that Vivian was the perfect wife. She made a profession out of being her husband's partner and public relations manager. My heart went out to her once I understood that she needed to control my open house because she didn't want Donn or me to fail.

My party concept must have looked like something out of the 1960s TV sitcom *The Beverly Hillbillies*. I pictured Jed, Granny, Elly May, and Jethro sitting at the fancy eatin' table (a billiard table), passing the possum stew to their guests on pot passers (cue sticks). When my guests left the party, a perfect ending would have been to shout, "Y'all come back now, ya hear?"

*   *   *

The church had an active young adult Sunday school group where I could interact with others my age who also had small children. What I found interesting was that some of the women would open the class not with scripture but with a reading from Kahlil Gibran's book *The Prophet*. It's an excellent book, especially the chapter on raising children, but I felt it wasn't appropriate for Christian Sunday school. At least not back then.

And then there was the time we talked in class about Jesus, and a man in his thirties confessed that he had no problem with the concept of God but didn't accept Jesus as God's son. I didn't know what to make of his comment. My relationship with Jesus kept me going; even so, his words gave me pause and have stayed with me all these years.

We had a lot of get-togethers at each other's houses and the church. We square danced in the church parking lot and had a men's and women's baseball team that played other churches in town. The women watched the kids from the sidelines when the men played, and vice versa. I was lousy at throwing a baseball, but I could catch, hit, and run fast.

On the evening of our last game, only nine players showed up. The score was five to four in our favor when Beth showed up right before the final inning. Our male coach approached me saying, "I know you've made three of the five runs tonight, but I feel like I have to put Beth in, and I know you're the only one I can bench who won't get mad at me. Do you mind?"

Yes, I mind! Tell your wife to sit out, or better yet, tell Beth to go home!

But I didn't say any of those things. I was the minister's wife and a Christian. I thought I was supposed to willingly sacrifice my joy so others could have theirs. But that didn't make me happy, especially when we lost the game.

In August 1977, we traded the Dodge Dart (also a lemon) for an Oldsmobile Cutlass Vista Cruiser station wagon. Michael went to a home day care close to an elementary school, where I started working as an assistant librarian, making $3.33 an hour. I also made $2.85 an hour as a lunch and playground supervisor.

The previous assistant librarian never took the time to put the new book cards into the card catalog. I worked on that task for four months while checking books in and out, replacing them on the shelves, and helping students find a book to read. Then I organized the media room, making a catalog of available films and educational games for the teachers who had no idea these resources existed.

I concluded that if my dream to be a music teacher didn't pan out, I could be content with spending my days surrounded by books and students who loved them as much as I did.

One of the older boys rushed into the library before school to tell me all about a movie he'd seen over the weekend. All I got from his gushing words were: Princess Leia, rescued by Han Solo and Luke Skywalker, bad guy Darth Vader, and Luke blew up a death star. The boy paused to catch his breath, then added, "It's the best movie I've ever seen!"

Although his elevator pitch was a bit sketchy, his excitement caused me to hire a sitter so Donn and I could see the movie. It was a thrilling, extraordinary film, not because it took place in space and an enormous ship flew over my head in the opening scene but because the underlying theme was spiritual: "May the Force Be with You!"

Luke didn't have to pray or beg for help. He just had to release his ego and trust the Force (power) already within him.

I loved this spirit world concept and wished it was true.

When the school year ended in 1978, I was pregnant with our second child and didn't sign up for another year at the school. That summer, Donn called during his camp counseling week to tell me he had decided to go to a seminary in Indianapolis, Indiana, for the fall semester. He would leave on Tuesday mornings, stay on campus for three nights, return on Friday afternoons, and work at the church on Saturdays, Sundays, and Mondays.

WHAT?

"You do remember that we're having a baby at the end of October, right?"

"Of course I do. The due date is on the weekend, and I'll be home. If you go into labor when I'm at the seminary, I'll only be two and a half hours away. That's plenty of time for me to get home if you call me when you have the first contraction."

"I won't have a car to get groceries or go to my prenatal appointments. And who will watch Michael when I'm at the doctor's?"

"We'll figure it out."

At this point in my life, I still couldn't stand up to my husband or anyone, for that matter. I was a failure with Vivian and didn't even try with the baseball coach.

Sometimes my mother would use silence to get her point across. Once, when my dad complained about getting leftovers for dinner, Mom picked up the serving plate and, without saying a word, opened the back door and tossed it into the backyard.

If only I had the guts to do something like that.

Dad didn't say anything, either. His silent comeback was to mow around it all summer. By September, it looked like lawn

74

art with a three-foot ring of grass around the plate. Had it been in an art gallery, I would have named it *The Wedding Ring*.

When Donn was home Friday afternoon through Monday, even though he had responsibilities at church, he made the most of the little time we had together. We actually had more *quality* family time than we'd ever had before. I had no problem finding people from the church willing to watch Michael and take me to my appointments, and I went to the grocery store on the weekends when I had the car.

However, I was perpetually tired with a rambunctious three-year-old in the house. After lunch, I would fall asleep while reading Michael a picture book. When my head began to drop, he'd say, "Mommy, don't close your eyes."

He balked at taking naps. I knew from experience that if I could get him to lie still for five minutes, he would fall asleep. One day, I was so tired I took him upstairs, laid him on my bed, and put my arm around him as best I could with a belly the size of a basketball taking up most of the space between us. I awoke alone on the bed to the sound of waterfalls.

This can't be good!

I ran down the hallway into the bathroom to find water cascading over the sink onto the floor. Michael was standing on his footstool in front of the basin, frantically turning the hot and cold water knobs back and forth in the same direction, inadvertently turning one knob off while at the same time turning the other one back on.

I stopped the floodgate, pulled every towel out of the linen closet to sop up the water before it escaped onto the hardwood floor in the hallway, then sat on the toilet seat and put my frightened child onto the little bit of lap I had left for him to sit on.

"I bet you were scared," I offered.

He nodded his little head.

"It's okay. It's just a little water. No big deal."

It wasn't a lot of water, but it was enough to make its way down the back wall of the coat closet on the first floor and into the basement. Thankfully, I knew to check and dry those areas before the water did any damage.

The baby, due the weekend before Halloween, never arrived, nor did it show up on Monday, October 30, or Tuesday, October 31, when Donn had to leave for Indianapolis.

A woman from the young adult group whose son was the same age as Michael called, offering to take us to the children's Halloween party at the church that evening. Children and adults were encouraged to come in costume. What does an overdue pregnant woman wear for a Halloween party? Her nun costume from her high school production of *The Sound of Music*, of course!

When I walked into the church basement for the party, people were shocked to see me. Not because I looked like a pregnant nun but because I still hadn't given birth.

"I thought you would have had the baby by now!"

"Me too!" I answered.

"How overdue are you?"

"Four days."

"Do you want a boy or a girl?"

"Girl."

I received even more looks at McDonald's when we walked in to get something to eat after the party. Was I in costume, or was I a pregnant nun with a three-year-old who calls me mommy?

On Thursday morning, November 2, Donn called to say his Friday class had been canceled. He arrived home that evening just a few hours before I had my first contraction. They were far apart, so we took some time before calling the person who offered to stay with Michael. Once we did call and were waiting for her arrival, the contractions suddenly picked up their pace. Ten minutes after arriving at the hospital, I told the nurse, "I need to push."

"You've only been in labor for a couple of hours. It's way too soon for that," the nurse insisted, flippantly turning her attention to take my pulse.

"I'm telling you I need to push. Have you called the doctor?"

Without looking up from her watch, she replied, "I'm sure he's on his way."

"Where is my husband?"

She finally looked at me. "Be patient. He's checking you in, and he'll have to change into scrubs before he's allowed in the room."

I was frustrated with her callous dismissal of me. When she finally put on gloves and got around to doing the internal exam, she shouted, "Oh my gosh! You're fully dilated! Don't push! Don't push!"

I wanted to scream, "No shit, lady!" but I was doing the Lamaze breathing to fight against pushing. Donn showed up as they rushed me to the delivery room.

"When can I push?" I asked as soon as my feet were in the stirrups.

"As soon as the doctor arrives."

"He's not here?"

"Am I too late?" The doctor asked as he rushed into the room.

I had been in labor for only three and a half hours and in the hospital for only forty-five minutes when our second child came into the world.

"It's a boy!" the doctor announced. "Just what you wanted, right?"

"Not exactly," I replied, disappointed. But when the nurse laid him in my arms, I fell in love with the little guy. His hands were too big to belong to a girl anyway. We named him Andrew.

Kentucky Again/ Roberts Chapel

1979 to 1980

Donn intended to finish his degree in Indianapolis, but his credits from Asbury Seminary wouldn't transfer. Returning to Kentucky to complete his last three semesters made more sense. So, in January of 1979, with two children, the youngest only two months old, we loaded up a U-Haul trailer during a snowstorm and headed back to Kentucky.

We lived in two apartments during the year and a half we were back in Nicholasville. The first apartment was a two-story fourplex with two walkout basement apartments. Our walkout had no windows on the east and south walls. The north wall housed two bedrooms and a living room, each with a small basement window that butted up to the ceiling. Only Donn was tall enough to look outside.

The only standard window was in the living room on the west wall near the front door. We discovered there wasn't a seal under that door when one morning, after a blustery winter storm, we woke up to find the three-foot-square entryway covered with an inch of snow.

When spring arrived, hundreds of bugs (I'm not exaggerating) wiggled through the ground-level window to parachute into the boys' bedroom and land on Michael's pillow. Luckily, he wasn't napping at the time. And then there were the super-hero roaches that wouldn't die no matter how hard or how many times we stomped on them. We learned to always look inside a drinking glass before filling it with water and taking a sip, especially at night.

Donn worked from 6:00 a.m. to 10:00 a.m. for Management Cleaning Controls cleaning floors at Sears. He polished, dust mopped, vacuumed, emptied trash, and sometimes did all-nighters stripping the waxed floors and rewaxing them. He got home with enough time to change clothes and get to his eleven o'clock class.

When he returned at 2:20, I headed out the door for my job at St. Joseph's Hospital making $3.48 an hour as a nurse assistant, rotating supplies in the operating rooms. The head nurse in surgery for the evening shift, a seminary student wife, was looking for another seminary spouse to carpool with and suggested I apply for the job.

Most surgeries were near completion when we got to the hospital for the 3:00 to 11:00 shift. My job was to restock the surgical supplies in the operating rooms that were recently cleaned, ensuring they had enough gloves, sutures, scal-pels, gauze, etc., for the next day and overnight emergency operations.

If I was done with my responsibilities and surgeries were still happening, I'd peek into the rooms to watch. I didn't have a good view, but it was something to do while I waited for the cleaning crew to finish up in the other rooms.

I remember the shock when I saw a doctor using a power drill like the one in my dad's toolbox to screw a pin into a woman's fractured hip. Once, a surgeon noticed me observing his patient's neck operation and said, "Grab a mask and come on in. You can look over my shoulder."

I jumped at the opportunity but didn't stay long. Looking inside a person's body was weird, especially when I saw the three-by-three-inch underside of her skin hanging off her neck.

One night, I walked into the OR, not realizing that the cleaning crew hadn't been there yet. Blood was scattered all over the floor. It was apparent that the surgical team had rushed back and forth through the blood to the supply closet to save the patient's life. I found out later the man had not survived.

That same night, after the room was cleaned and no more surgeries were scheduled, all the OR and hallway lights were turned off, which was creepy after the recent death. The only lights on the floor were in the office and the women's locker room, where I would express milk into a baby bottle for my nursing four-month-old, who was under the care of his father in the evening while I worked.

Donn and I passed each other in the night. He was asleep when I returned home at midnight. I was sleeping when he left for work before sunrise. I nursed Andrew before leaving the house in the afternoon and again when I got home. However, when I was at work, the baby refused to take that same milk from a bottle.

During the second week of my employment, Donn called me at the hospital in desperation. "Andrew still won't take the bottle, and all he does is cry. Our children are more important than seminary. I can't get any studying done anyway. I will quit and get a full-time job if you leave your job."

I left a beautiful home in Illinois and moved back to Kentucky so Donn could finish his theology degree. The last thing I wanted was for him to quit. Trusting that another job with better hours would come my way, I turned in my resignation and left at the end of the week.

My friend Dee, who now had three children, offered me a job cleaning her house once a week. She also paid a sitter to watch our five children at the church so she could help Howard in the church office, giving us both alone time without children. Her generosity went above and beyond.

Donn took on another job on Sunday evenings as a youth pastor and pianist for a church congregation in Lexington. He also gave singing lessons to several church teens on Saturday afternoons at their homes.

In June, through another seminary wife needing a carpooler, I got a full-time job making $3.50 an hour in the Word Processing Department at Kentucky Central Life Insurance in Lexington. During the week, the boys rode with Donn to the seminary, where he dropped them off at the campus daycare. Another seminary wife from Illinois who worked at the daycare got to witness Andrew's first steps instead of me.

In high school, I learned how to type on a manual typewriter using carbon paper to make copies and an eraser to correct mistakes. The school also had a couple of 1961 IBM Selectric typewriters, which used correction tape for fixing errors. This was a big WOW for typists.

The Word Processing Department at my new job used the 1973 new solid-state IBM Mag Card Selectric II with an electronic memory of eight thousand typewritten characters! This was futuristic!

The customer service department dictated letters on a magnetic device and sent their recorded tape to our department for transcribing. I would slide a three-by-seven-inch Mylar-based magnetic card into a console connected to my typewriter. Every character I typed while listening to the tape was recorded in the typewriter's memory and on the card. If I made a mistake, I'd hit the backspace key to erase the error on the page and the card. Even though eleven women typing in the same room made for a noisy day, I was thrilled to use this exciting new technology.

I had only been employed for a few months when the company moved into the brand-new Kincaid Towers, a 333-foot-high, twenty-two-story high-rise building in downtown Lexington, just a few blocks from our old office. Kentucky Central took up the top thirteen floors. I was on floor seventeen with a fabulous view of the city.

Sadly, a year before my employment, the unfinished Kincaid Towers was used for filming the movie *Steel*, where Stuntman A. J. Bakunas died when the airbag he landed on ruptured after a stunt fall from one of the top floors. Several of my coworkers saw it happen. Their retelling has stayed with me every time I remember this job.

One day, a coworker handed me the book *Illusions: The Adventures of a Reluctant Messiah* by Richard Bach. It was a fascinating tale of Donald, who quits his messiah job to travel around the country and give people rides in his biplane. He meets another biplane pilot, Richard, a disillusioned writer, and they form a teacher-student relationship. Donald gives Richard the messiah manual, showing him how to remove limits from his thoughts by looking at the world from a higher perspective. Richard eventually learns how to walk on water.

I was pretty taken with this book that randomly came into my life. I could identify with Jesus, the rebel, burned out and walking away from his job, tired of crowds always wanting something from him. Maybe the man at our last church who couldn't accept Jesus as God's son was on the right track. Maybe Jesus was just a human who understood that life is an illusion. And if so, perhaps that is why he said we could do the same work he did and even greater ones. It was certainly food for thought.

On November 4, 1979, Iranian students stormed the U.S. Embassy in Tehran and took sixty Americans hostage. The event was all my coworkers talked about that following week. Some were so scared they thought the United States would be bombed and we'd all die.

I was concerned about what was happening in Tehran, but I had more important things to do when I got home than watching the news, like cooking, playtime, bath time, and tucking my children into bed. So, when two terrified coworkers came to me for reassurance because I was a minister's wife, I said something profound like, "Worry isn't going to change what's happening in Tehran."

I wish I had locked my lips after speaking, but the next thing out of my mouth was, "I don't know about you, but I'm not worried. If I die, I know where I'm going."

I remember feeling clever for tacking on that remark until much later in life when I realized it wasn't reassuring or helpful; it was disrespectful and arrogant. Basically, I told them they were going to hell if they weren't Christians. All I did that day was give them something new to worry about. There should be a legal requirement that all Christians be licensed before witnessing to others.

At the same time I started the Kentucky Central job, Donn was given a student pastorate position at Roberts Chapel, a United Methodist Church built in 1845. It was once used as a military hospital during the Civil War due to its location just a few miles north of Camp Nelson. In 1984, Roberts Chapel was added to the National Register of Historic Places.

The red brick building housed a large sanctuary with two aisles, three sections of pews, and two coal-burning stoves midway down the two aisles. With only ten to twelve people in attendance, only one stove was lit during winter. The small congregation, my boys, and I huddled close enough to the heated stove to keep our feet and hands warm but not too close for the heat to put us to sleep. By the end of the service, our faces were hot and our bottoms cold. Even in warm weather when the stoves weren't heating, we all sat in the same place as Donn preached from the pulpit thirty-five feet away. What can I say? It was our spot.

It took all my strength to keep Andrew's wiggly little body on the pew. He crawled, but I couldn't let him crawl on the coal-sooted sanctuary floor. The church had a newer education building attached to the back side of the sanctuary heated with gas, but the flooring was cold tile. I let Andrew scramble around on the floor in the only carpeted Sunday school room while I taught Michael and any random children who were spending the weekend with their grandparents.

Now that Donn and I had better jobs, he quit polishing floors at Sears. We also broke our rental lease on the bug-infested apartment and moved into a roomy duplex with a good landlord and two seminary students who lived in the other unit. When they moved out, two drug dealers moved in.

Okay, I confess. I don't know if our neighbors were drug dealers, but visitors came and left at all hours of the day and night, staying for only a few minutes. Maybe their guests were picking up their Mary Kay cosmetics.

In the spring of 1980, the drug dealers moved out of the duplex, and a refugee family from Laos, who didn't speak English, moved in. A local church sponsored them, bringing them to the U.S. after a Communist government came to power in their country. The family spent their first night turning the water on and off in their bathtub, eight feet from our bedroom. It didn't bother us. We figured they didn't have indoor plumbing in Laos, which their host family confirmed the next day.

One afternoon, I was in the front yard getting the mail when the school bus dropped off their oldest child. He was just a few years older than Michael, who was almost five.

The driver stepped off the bus and walked toward me. "Would you please tell the host family that the boy's father gave him a hundred-dollar bill for his school lunch, and the change is in the boy's pocket?"

"Oh my gosh! Of course!" I relayed the message as soon as the sponsor arrived.

Michael and their oldest child played outside like best friends even though they didn't speak the same language. One warm day when I was in the backyard watching my kids and theirs, the father came over to where I was sitting, pointed to an English word in his Laotian/English dictionary, and lifted his eyebrows with a smile.

I understood what he wanted. I said the word out loud, "Automobile."

"Automobile," he repeated. We did that over and over with several words. He then stood, put both hands on the dictionary, gave me a nod, which I understood as thank you, and returned to his apartment. I understood better how the children could play without using words.

Seminary graduation was approaching but wasn't coming fast enough for me. Our nomad life was taking a toll on both of us. In our eight years of marriage, we'd moved eight times, sometimes twice a year, and money was always a concern. We had our music ministry to fall back on for extra cash, but that slowed down after we had children.

Our lifestyle was affecting the kids, too. One time when my mother came to visit, she took the boys shopping. When she pulled out her wallet at the checkout counter, Michael said in his sweet voice, "Don't spend all the money, Grandma; we need it." Of course, he didn't know she was spending her own money. Thank you, Mom!

Our family desperately needed stability, which, for me, was Donn with one full-time, decent-paying job and a nice house that we could live in for longer than six months to a year. I tried to always make the best of whatever life handed me, but even Positive Pollyanna had her dark days.

I had two small children and only one car. There were no parents or in-laws nearby to help with the kids or keep them overnight for the weekend. When I wasn't working, I was at home, ensuring everyone's needs were met while sacrificing my own. I felt lucky just to get time alone in the bathroom! On Saturday afternoons, when Donn was in Lexington giving music lessons and the boys were napping, I'd sit on that scratchy green sofa and sob into a pillow. It was the only time I had by myself.

Those grim Saturday afternoons felt like one of those dreams where you desperately need to run, but your legs won't move. The marriage-for-life rule felt like a prison with no hope of parole. I didn't know how to change my circumstances, so I accepted this freedomless existence with a smile like a good Christian woman while secretly hoping that life was just an illusion, as Richard Bach suggested. I didn't want to walk on water, swim in the dirt, or walk through walls. I just wanted to see through the illusion and take control of my life.

That day would eventually come, but it would take time and many more books to get there.

Perry/Baylis/Fishhook
1980 to 1983

In June of 1980, when Donn's seminary graduation was finally behind us, we moved to west central Illinois, where the conference appointed Donn to a three-point charge (three churches). I was now three hundred miles away from my family instead of four hundred fifty miles. Closer but not convenient for a day visit or a spur-of-the-moment grandchild sleepover.

We lived in Perry (population 480). Donn also served the church in Baylis (population 300) and, twice a month, preached at Fishhook, a tiny country church in an unincorporated town off the main highway that reminded me of a little country schoolhouse.

Donn had an office in the Perry church next to our house. He didn't make much money, twelve thousand a year, but since we didn't pay rent, only utilities, it was enough so I could stay home. We had a large two-car garage nestled between the house and church, and most days, I had full access to our station wagon to drive twenty minutes south to Pittsfield (population 4,000) for doctor's appointments and groceries.

Perry had a lot going on for such a small town: a post office, a Masonic Temple, a tiny grocery store, a popular restaurant, a meat-packing store, an elementary school, a gas station, auto repair, several churches, and an eight-lane bowling alley.

Donn and I bowled on a Friday night couples league with young newlyweds. To accommodate sixteen teams, we played at either 6:00 p.m. or 9:00 p.m. If we bowled the first shift, our teammates came to our house afterward to play cards. Gretchen, a tall, high school redhead from our church with freckles and a lovely personality, watched our boys every Friday night during the bowling season.

I exercised at the church once a week with other stay-at-home moms. Our preschool children played in the nursery while we sweated to Jane Fonda's *Workout* and *Jazzercise* records.

The church was very active. Besides the Sunday service, Sunday school, and Bible school, there was an annual mother-daughter banquet and a basement sale. Of course, I helped with all events. I remember one sale when a woman who rarely came to Sunday services showed up to help with pricing and started inflating the prices already tagged. Her excuse was, "It's for the church. We should charge more."

I thought the smarter way to bring in money was for members to throw an extra dollar into the offering every Sunday. If twenty people did that for fifty-two weeks a year, the church would make double what the sale brought in, and the women wouldn't have to bust their buns putting it together.

The parsonage in Perry was old but in better condition than our first house. It had two bedrooms downstairs—a small one for the boys with a window that faced the front porch and a good-sized one for us—plus two bedrooms upstairs in the heated attic area.

The large farmhouse kitchen desperately needed updating. The door to the sunroom was on the south wall next to six feet of built-in plywood cabinets. The north wall had a refrigerator and empty wall space. The stove sat on the west wall between two long windows and more open wall space.

In the middle of the long east wall stood a five-foot-wide antique, white cast-iron single sink with a drainboard on a white metal cabinet. (This was the second house with an antique sink.) The bathroom door was on its right, and the mudroom/laundry room door was on its left.

The outside entrance into the mudroom, which faced the church and our driveway, didn't have a lock on the door. When members stopped by the house, they walked into our laundry room and knocked on the kitchen door.

One afternoon after mowing the lawn and showering, Donn opened the mudroom door to toss his towel into the hamper and discovered a church member with her hand in the air, ready to knock on the door. Familiar with his showering routine, I suspected he was naked, so when I heard voices, I hurried into the kitchen, where I found him hiding behind the kitchen door, his head peeking around the door, calmly conversing with a female church member. Hilarious!

By December, I had a new kitchen with plenty of counter space, new cabinets covering three walls, and a window above the sink. I helped with the plan and picked the cabinets and the countertop. We had new cabinets but not new appliances.

Directly behind the house were two old walnut trees with a clothesline stretched between them. There's nothing better than slipping into bed with the smell of clean sheets fresh off the clothesline. When the weather was good, I air-dried all our clothing, towels, and sheets except for Donn's underwear. He didn't want them hangin' in the breeze for the whole town to see. I stopped using the clothesline in the fall after a tennis-ball-sized walnut almost landed on my head.

I didn't realize then that those trees were responsible for my yearly cough and laryngitis. On the bright side, my children behaved better when I couldn't speak. Rather than shouting from the next room, I had to get close to them and whisper, "It's time for you to get ready for bed," or "It's time to wash hands for dinner." Amazingly, without argument, they obeyed. If only I could have remembered to whisper when my voice was working properly.

In 1981, the housing market crashed. Home sales and the number of new homes built had plummeted by 50 percent. The interest rate on a thirty-year mortgage rose to a high of 18.45 percent. It didn't matter to us because we lived in a rent-free parsonage, but it did affect my parents.

After Admiral sold the factory and moved their business to Taiwan, my parents moved to Rockford, Illinois. Dad continued to build residential homes, Mom became a real estate agent, and then the market crashed. Few houses were being built or sold.

During Mom's weekly phone call, she announced, "We're moving to Florida."

What? I just moved back to Illinois!

I'd seen my parents twice in the seven months after moving to Perry, and now, they would be a thousand miles away. I couldn't catch a break.

Timeshare was a booming business in the 1980s. In Florida, Dad turned ocean-side hotels into timeshare condos, and Mom sold them. A timeshare works like this: rather than buying a vacation house or condo, you buy a week, or several weeks, in a timeshare and share the cost of that unit with others who also bought a week in that unit. You can vacation yearly at that location or exchange your week for a comparable unit in a timeshare resort anywhere in the world.

Even though Mom's job was to get people to buy into the timeshare concept, she did everything she could to ensure they knew what they were getting into, especially young couples. She felt a timeshare was too much of a financial risk for them.

I wasn't as upset that my parents were far away as I thought I'd be. I was too busy raising children to ponder the miles between us, and after eight years, I realized I'd become accustomed to not seeing family. Plus, I had friendly people around me all the time. The rooms in our house all had heat, I wasn't stomping on roaches, and my bedroom wasn't in the dining room. All things considered, my life was going pretty well.

Donn was available more often, except for two weeks every summer when he went to the annual conference meeting in June and church camp in July. I was okay with him being gone but didn't appreciate being left without transportation or that he got two weeks away from parenting when I only got Friday nights during bowling season.

One summer, while Donn was gone, the tire swing in our side yard hit Michael, age six, on the side of the head, and his ear and cheek swelled to twice their size. With no vehicle, I called two members, one to watch Andrew and another to take Michael and me to the emergency room in Pittsfield. Except for the swelling, he was fine. When we returned home, I wrapped an ice pack in a towel and tied it to his head.

On Sunday mornings, Donn left early to preach at the other two churches. We didn't see him again until after Sunday school when he arrived in Perry for his third service. That same summer, when Michael went to the ER, Andrew, age three, wanted to help make breakfast on Sunday morning. I wouldn't let him stir the Cream of Wheat while it was cooking on the stove, but after I poured it into three bowls on the counter, I allowed him to stand on a chair and stir in the sugar and butter. While mixing, he accidentally stepped sideways off the chair, hitting the left side of his head on the sharp corner of the old stove. Two children, two head injuries in the same year.

When I washed the blood off and saw a hole through the upper part of his ear, I again called two church members, one to watch Michael and take him to Sunday school and one to take Andrew and me to the emergency room. The doctor, concerned that Andrew would pull on his ear, wrapped a large bandage around his head. He looked like a tiny, injured soldier just home from the Civil War.

When we arrived home, Sunday school had ended, and the church service was about to begin. Andrew was alert and felt fine, so I took him to the church nursery, explaining to the volunteer teacher what had happened before I headed to the sanctuary.

When it was time for the children's message, all the kids, including those in the nursery, made their way down the aisle to the front of the church for their time with the pastor. Gasps came from the congregation as they watched a head-bandaged Andrew happily bouncing down the aisle to where his father stood, wide-eyed and speechless.

Seeing his son smiling and acting normal, Donn chuckled, "Well, something happened to you since I saw you last! I can't wait to hear all about it," he said, inquisitively looking at me along with everyone else in the sanctuary.

I smiled and shrugged my shoulders. What else could I do? The kids were waiting for Donn to talk, not me.

When I wasn't cleaning, cooking, or at the ER with children, I had my nose in a book. I went through all the Agatha Christie mysteries I could get my hands on, and then a church member introduced me to The White Indian Series by Donald Clayton Porter. The first book, *White Indian: The Lusty Turbulent Saga of America's First Frontier*, came out in 1979. It was hot and sexy. I read more now than ever before.

And then other people started handing me what I called "out-of-the-box" books. The first book was Shirley MacLaine's controversial 1983 memoir *Out on a Limb*, in which she shared her spiritual quest during her mid-forties after asking herself, "Who am I?"

I found her journey as fascinating as Richard Bach's *Illusions* book. Her quest included reading every metaphysical book she could get her hands on, with a special interest in reincarnation, the eternal life of the soul, mediumship, and a connection with her higher self.

The second book was *Edgar Cayce—The Sleeping Prophet: The Monumental Story of the Life, the Prophecies, and the Astounding Medical "Readings" of America's Greatest Mystic!* by Jess Stearn. While unconscious, Cayce placed his mind in contact with the universal consciousness and responded to questions asked of him. He diagnosed illnesses and answered questions on reincarnation, dreams, the afterlife, past lives, nutrition, empowerment, personal growth, auras, and more.

I was amazed that Cayce was a devout Christian and Sunday school teacher. His psychic abilities came to him around age ten, when he first began to read the Bible from cover to cover. He continued this practice every year until he died in 1945 at age sixty-seven. I wrestled with the fact that if the most documented psychic of the twentieth century had been a dedicated Christian his entire life, why would the church pooh-pooh psychic abilities to the point where they were now considered evil instead of a gift?

When I heard that Christians were banning the 1982 book *Holy Blood, Holy Grail* by Michael Baigent, Richard Leigh, and Henry Lincoln, I went to the Pittsfield library and put my name on a waiting list. This nonfiction 1982 book suggests that the Holy Grail refers to a bloodline that goes back to Jesus and Mary Magdalene. The book is listed as one of the most controversial books of the 1980s. Dan Brown used it in 2003 as a reference for his fictional book *The Da Vinci Code*, which eventually introduced the concept to millions of readers and moviegoers that Jesus was married and had children.

Christians were getting their panties in a wad over this book. The theory made perfect sense to me. Jesus was male. Mary was female. Why wouldn't Jesus go forth and reproduce like everyone else? Although I found all the ideas in these books intriguing and food for thought, my life was filled to the brim with church obligations, a husband, two children, and a third one on the way.

As my February due date grew near, women in the church would say things like, "Wouldn't it be wonderful after two boys if you got a little girl? Maybe you'll get her on Valentine's Day."

"Another boy would be wonderful, too," I would lie. I knew I would love him wholeheartedly if we had another boy. But deep down inside, I was afraid I would be disappointed, so I tried to convince myself that I didn't want a girl.

When I heard that a friend, another Methodist clergy wife, had given birth in the back seat of their car, I was in a panic. Michael arrived in five and a half hours. Andrew showed up in three and a half. What if the next child appeared en route to the hospital?

I stored clean plastic sheeting in the car to sit on in case my water broke or I had to give birth there. I imagined our red station wagon on the side of the road with the tailgate raised and my legs spread apart in full view for travelers to witness the birthing process.

When I told my doctor how worried I was, he said, "Call the hospital when you have your first contraction and tell them Speedy is on her way. Then get here as fast as possible without breaking the speed limit."

I went into labor at six o'clock in the morning on February 12, 1982, Abraham Lincoln's birthday (a big deal in Illinois). By the time we got the boys up and dressed, called the hospital, dropped off the boys at the neighbor's, drove to the hospital (I sat on the sheet), and got settled in the triage room, the contractions sped up just like with Andrew.

They rushed me to a delivery room prepared for a woman who had been waiting to give birth for ten hours. When our baby was born, the doctor excitedly announced, "It's a girl!"

Shocked, I babbled, "A girl? Are you sure?"

The doctor laughed out loud, "Yes, I'm sure!"

It took only three hours of labor for Karen to complete our family.

In week two, Karen had thrush, an oral yeast infection common for newborns. By week four, she had lost all the weight she had gained after birth and had a cough, a rash, and pneumonia. The doctor prescribed antibiotics and told me to supplement nursing with formula, which I did immediately. That night, I lay on the floor beside Karen's crib, listening to her labored breathing, afraid to leave her.

The formula was a lifesaver for Karen and for me. Having visible confirmation that she drank all the formula gave me peace of mind. For Karen's health and my sanity, I stopped nursing entirely, and she quickly regained her weight.

One evening as I rocked her to sleep, her breath gently caressing my neck, I fondly reminisced about all the years I sat like this with her brothers on my shoulder. My heart soared with love for my children. And then, unexpectedly, I had a moment of clarity about my future. I knew, without a doubt, that I would never become a school music teacher. Tears dripped down my cheeks as I mourned the loss of my dream.

At my six-week postpartum exam, the doctor said, "You're pregnant."

Frozen, I stared back in disbelief.

"I'm joking," he laughed.

Not funny!

"How are things going at your house with three kids?"

"It's stressful at times," I confessed.

"Lock yourself in a closet for thirty minutes," he advised.

Surely he was joking again. This time I chuckled, "I'd be arrested for negligence."

"Then put your kids in the closet."

What is wrong with this guy?

Serious now, I countered, "Then I'll be arrested for child abuse."

When I got home, I immediately secured a new doctor.

At three months, Karen was coughing a lot. Thinking it was caused by allergies, the new doctor put her on soy-based formula. Donn's low salary qualified us for the Illinois food assistance program for women, infants, and children (WIC).

Thankfully, the more expensive soy formula was on the free food list, along with eggs, milk, juice, cheese, bread, peanut butter, and low-sugar cereals.

Karen was almost crawling, and my parents, now settled in Florida, hadn't seen her for six months. They were busy with their new jobs and couldn't take time off from work. We didn't have the time or the funds to pay for meals, hotels, and gas to drive to and from Florida.

Then one morning, right in front of me on the kitchen table, the solution was on the back of a cereal box, "Kids Fly Free one way (age two to sixteen) with five box tops if accompanied by an adult."

The recession that caused my parents to move to Florida also caused a slump in airline industry revenue, creating an airfare war. Rather than giving discounts, one innovative airline joined forces with a cereal company and conceived the boxtop idea. It certainly got my attention.

We could have our first family trip AND see Mom and Dad!

I only had two cereal boxes in the house at any moment because I made a hot breakfast every day except for Saturday. Although money was tight, I bought eighteen boxes of cereal (some of them with my WIC coupons), giving us ten box tops each for Michael and Andrew to fly round trip. Karen was young enough to fly for free.

On Friday, October 8, we drove two hours to the St. Louis Lambert International Airport to catch our flight. I scheduled our return flight for Columbus Day the following Monday, so Michael only missed one school day.

Passengers spoke in whispers as the plane took off. Michael, who was six, was in the aisle seat on my right. Donn was across the aisle. Karen was in my lap next to Andrew, now four, who sat in the window seat. He was unusually quiet as he looked out the window during takeoff. When the plane took a steep bank to the left, he calmly but loudly asked, "Are we gonna crash now?" Laughter erupted throughout the aircraft. My children have always been entertaining.

So many times, we think that we can't have something we want. But if we pay attention, the solution is usually right in front of us. In this instance, cereal box tops gave us a family vacation. And then, a month after we returned from Florida, my parents' boss offered them the same jobs but in Gatlinburg, Tennessee.

For the next twelve years, we vacationed at my parents' condo for one week every summer, with free room and board, a swimming pool, and a hot tub in the Great Smoky Mountains—one of the most charming and fun getaways in the United States.

The greatest gift, though, was the extended family bonding time. I didn't need my parents as much as I did early on in life, but after loading the car and saying our goodbyes to head back to Illinois, I'd sit in the front seat holding back tears as we drove away.

Life was better now that we were settled in a town and a home, but I was still dissatisfied with our marriage and disenchanted with being a clergy spouse. I adored my children, but at least once a month, I would get overwhelmed and frustrated with them.

The conference had a counselor available to clergy families free of charge. After telling him what was happening, he said, "Have you ever heard of premenstrual syndrome?"

PMS causes physical and emotional symptoms after a woman ovulates and before she starts her menstrual period because that's when estrogen and progesterone levels fall if she's not pregnant. My once-a-month physical symptom was a headache; the emotional symptoms were irritability, tension, and mood swings.

I had never heard of PMS because it wasn't considered a "real" medical problem until the 1980s. Before that time, the medical field believed it was just a social problem. When I understood what was happening in my body, I was able to deal with the symptoms. Having confirmation that I didn't dislike my children once a month was also a big help.

The counselor added, "It sounds like you have the curse of competency. You can do whatever you put your mind to, and you are a perfectionist, so you go above and beyond what is expected. I suggest you focus on your children and ensure you get time for yourself." He leaned in with a wink and added, "I guarantee the church will survive without you."

Interesting! He didn't suggest I focus on my husband like a good Christian woman. I appreciated that.

The last year I taught Bible school in Perry, the teacher's curriculum (non-Methodist) called for me to teach the pledge of allegiance to the Bible. I had no idea there was such a pledge, and when I read it, I couldn't in good conscience teach it.

I wasn't at a place in my life yet where I questioned everything, but I knew from studying and teaching the Bible for ten years that there were too many contradictions for me to teach children that every word in the Bible was crafted by God.

Then one Sunday, I noticed a new banner on the sanctuary wall that disturbed me. It read:

Jesus First.
Others Second.
Yourself last.

Women had been the worker bees in every church I'd attended. They didn't need the JOY reminder; they naturally put themselves last, sacrificing their needs for everyone else's. I enjoyed helping others but also resented feeling obligated to say yes when I wanted to say no.

We are told to love our neighbor as ourselves, which means we must first love—ourselves. It's like the airline telling us to put on our masks before helping others with theirs. It isn't selfish. It's necessary for the survival of those around us. We can't help anyone if we can't breathe or are burned out, stressed, or resentful.

At this point, I didn't know how to put myself first. I didn't even know who I was. But thankfully, I was starting to think for myself. It was about time!

PART TWO

Finding Myself

Neponset/Mineral
1983 to 1986

IN JUNE OF 1983, I ATTEMPTED to pack the kitchen for our next move, but my annual congestion, croupy cough, and laryngitis were getting the best of me. The moving van was arriving the following day, and I was way behind schedule when Barb, the Methodist minister's wife from the next town, stopped by.

"I'm here to help in any way I can. What do you need me to do?" she asked.

With a cough that sounded like a dog's bark, I tried to answer.

"Oh my goodness, you're sick! Sit down right now," she ordered.

I sat like an obedient dog.

"Have you been to the doctor?"

"*Bark*, have a *bark*, appointment in, *bark*, an hour."

"Where's Donn?"

"Office, *bark*, packing."

"I'll stay here with the kids and finish the kitchen. Get ready to leave, and don't worry about a thing!"

When I returned three hours later, the kitchen and office were packed, and Donn was home. I took the prescribed antibiotic and cough medicines and went to bed in a medicated bliss.

* * *

Our next appointment was a two-point charge (two churches), about three hours northeast in central Illinois. The smaller church, located in Mineral, a village with a population of 325, was a fourteen-minute drive on a county backroad. Neponset, the town we would live in, had a population of 575.

The parsonage was a large, older two-story building. Counting the attic and the basement, it had four floors with landings on all the staircases. The attic had windows, flooring, many shelves for storage, and plenty of head space. The second floor boasted four large bedrooms with beautiful hardwood floors and a walk-in closet in the master bedroom.

The carpeted living and dining rooms on the main level overflowed with sunshine from three substantial picture windows that filled three walls, one on the east and two on the south. Off the front entrance, we turned a nine-foot-by-nine-foot room with French doors into a playroom. The front porch covered the entire east side of the house, facing the elementary school playground across the street. A two-car detached garage sat behind the house.

The large kitchen had a wide window above the sink overlooking the south side of the church and our side yard, where I could watch the children playing while I prepared meals.

The kitchen was huge because it was extended onto the back porch a few years earlier. I never understood why they didn't also update the kitchen workspace that took up one small corner of the room and had old plywood cabinets and an old laminate countertop. Instead, they added a half bathroom which had no heat.

When we visited with the Pastor Parish Committee two months earlier and took a tour of the house, the previous minister's wife pulled me aside in the kitchen, whispering, "In the winter, I store my potatoes in the bathroom. It's too cold in there to do anything else, if you get my drift."

What's up with parsonages and unheated rooms?

The bathroom upstairs was delightfully quaint, with a claw-foot tub, but it didn't have a shower. There was a showerhead in the basement but no stall, not even a curtain. I was not going down two flights of stairs to stand on a cold concrete floor and shower in full view of whoever wandered down to the basement, such as the water softener guy. By autumn, a three-foot-by-three-foot shower stall with a plastic curtain made a home in our kitchen bathroom, but there was still no heat. *Brrr!*

Outside we had three apple trees, Concorde grapevines, raspberries, blackberries, rhubarb, and a garden with vegetables ready for picking that took up more acreage than our last house. As if I didn't already have my hands full unpacking and keeping an eye on children, I now had to find time to keep an eye on produce.

I had two hours every afternoon in the summer heat while two-year-old Karen napped to process all those veggies in a kitchen without air conditioning.

I learned how to make pickles, rhubarb pie, and rhubarb cake during the first two months. I canned tomatoes and green beans and dug up potatoes, radishes, and carrots, serving as many vegetables as possible at mealtimes. When we took a short vacation to see my parents, I came home to cucumbers the size of footballs.

In the fall, I made grape jelly and apple pies. Some of the produce rotted on the vine. If it hadn't been for the 1971 Betty Crocker cookbook Mom gave me when I got married, the whole garden would have died.

The following spring, I allowed the grass to grow over the garden and invited the congregation to pick as many grapes and apples as they wanted, but the berries and rhubarb were off-limits. They were mine for breakfast!

Even so, I loved the house with its large rooms and front porch, affording easy access to the elementary school and playground equipment across the street. I loved the town, too. I could walk anywhere. Two minutes to the public library. Four minutes to the small grocery store, the post office, and the bank that contacted us to make a deposit if one of our checks was about to bounce. Being a minister's family has its perks.

The town was perfect for raising children. My dream was to stay there for a long time.

*　*　*

Every church has its own personality, and all good ministers know, at least they should, that they are there to help facilitate the church's mission, not try to change it. Donn was one of those good ministers, yet there was conflict from the first month.

At the first board meeting, they asked Donn to visit members in nursing homes and also the homebound. At the next board meeting, they complained that his visits cost them too much travel mileage.

On the Fourth of July, I answered the house telephone and heard an angry male voice asking, "Why didn't the minister ring the church bell today?"

I thought the man was a board member, so I asked, "Is that something he was supposed to do?"

Shouting into the phone, the man yelled, "He always rings the bell on Independence Day."

The man thought he was talking to the previous minister's wife, so I nicely replied, "My husband is the new minister. He's only been here three weeks. Would you like to speak with him?"

Instead of responding, the man hung up. According to the board, ringing the bell was something the last minister chose to do. Donn was not expected to follow suit.

And then, I was targeted. At least, that's how it felt.

I offered to play the piano with the organist at Sunday services, and she said okay. The two instruments added more energy to the service, and many people told me they enjoyed the addition of the piano.

The organist, however, told the board that people complained the piano was drowning out the pipe organ (which is impossible) and requested a written rule that no one could play the piano with the organ unless she personally invited them. She must have had enough board members who were family (or were scared of her), so the motion passed.

Afterward, my neighbor, who voted no, responded, "I can't believe the board just said Gaye can't play the piano in our church."

Shortly after, the choir director retired and appointed me as her replacement. A few board members voted against me, but I got the job anyway. Choir practice was filled with tension. The organist wouldn't talk to me, and when I asked her to change the tempo or volume, she did so with a glare. I carefully worded everything I said to avoid conflict.

The second summer, a woman in charge of Bible school tried to guilt me into teaching. "We don't have enough teachers. If you don't help, we'll have to cancel."

I was surprised that I stood my ground on this one. "This is the first year all my kids are old enough to attend Bible school. I could have five evenings alone. That's something I haven't had for eleven years."

"But Karen is too young for Bible school. There is a nursery, but it's only for children whose parents are helping," she countered.

Both of my arms flew up in the air. "That's perfect! Her father will be there the whole time."

Those five nights were delicious. I read on our front porch and sang my heart out while playing our piano—alone—in my house. *Yay!*

Another woman stopped by the parsonage, handed me a jewelry box, and with an excited smile, announced, "I noticed you never wear a necklace to church, so I bought one for you."

I was offended that she assumed I didn't own any jewelry. I didn't wear shiny objects around my neck on Sunday because they were bait for the littlest children to grab and break.

Thankfully, books seem to have a way of finding me. As I browsed the shelves of the Christian Bookstore, *Well-Intentioned Dragons: Ministering to Problem People in the Church* by Marshall Shelley jumped out at me.

The book's premise was that every church has well-meaning people who don't intend to be difficult, even though they often are. The book confirmed that when a minister or anyone in ministry feels attacked, it causes them to question their calling.

I loved singing in church, enjoyed teaching Sunday school, and genuinely cared for others, so I tried to see those few fire-breathing dragons as people who just wanted the best for their church. However, I became increasingly embittered with every conflict. Underneath my Pollyanna smile, the current pressure, coupled with fifteen years of discontent, was on the verge of eruption.

Christians, Bah Humbug!

At the end of January 1985, I was thirty-one years old. Our children were nine, six, and almost three when Donn went on a men's spiritual renewal retreat called Walk to Emmaus (*uh-mey-uhs*). The event ran from Thursday evening to Sunday evening. I was scheduled to attend the women's retreat the following weekend.

This three-day course in Christianity is meant to inspire, challenge, and equip local church members for Christian action in their homes, churches, and communities. Walk to Emmaus refers to when Jesus appears to two of his followers after his resurrection as they walk to the village of Emmaus.

Donn left for the retreat mid-afternoon on Thursday. His retreat sponsor drove an hour north to pick him up and then two hours south to the retreat center. I planned on visiting my sister Melody at her home northwest of Chicago for the weekend so our kids could play together, but that evening, we had a blizzard that closed all the highways in northern Illinois.

School closed on Friday, leaving the kids and me trapped at home without cable TV. Thankfully, we still had electricity, heat, and the VCR tape of *The NeverEnding Story* for them to watch while I went outside to shovel snow. Although it was freezing, the brisk fresh air and exercise felt good.

I shoveled the sidewalk toward the house south of us, owned by a lovely older couple who attended the church and were surrogate grandparents for our children. I shoveled their front walk and porch with loving thoughts, but as I turned to shovel the walk toward the church north of us, I was once again angry at the dragons and mad at Donn for getting spiritual over the weekend while I was getting frostbite.

The more I thought about my upcoming retreat, the more I didn't want to go. The only thing I knew about the event was that I would have a roommate and couldn't wear my watch.

I envisioned checking in Thursday night and coming up against a woman with a twitchy lip and raspy gangster voice saying, "Hand over your watch, honey."

I saw myself wrestling her to the floor as she tried to wrangle the timepiece off my wrist, then walking out the door and driving to the nearest Holiday Inn, where I would soak in a hot tub with scented candles lighting the room as the swirling water massaged my naked body. *Ahhhh!*

But then I remembered I would be riding with our sponsor, who would again drive an hour north, pick me up and drive two hours south. What a waste of gasoline! He was taking this Christian love and sacrifice stuff a little too far.

Donn returned from his weekend and assured me, "No one collects watches. They suggest you leave it in your suitcase. You won't need it anyway. In the morning, someone will play music in the hallways to wake you up and ring a little bell when it's time to head out."

So, if I oversleep, a happy Christian will enter my room and ring a little bell in my ear? Give me a break!

I knew I didn't have the right attitude to be at this Christian event. I was positive that sometime during the weekend, one of those happy Christians would pull me aside and tell me I was going to hell if I didn't straighten up.

As the weekend grew closer, I decided I could use a weekend out of town, and if I didn't like the retreat, I would walk to the Holiday Inn. Unfortunately, the event center was out of town, eight miles from the closest hotel. *Drat!*

When I arrived, no one tried to take my watch. At seven o'clock in the evening, our sponsors started applauding as we were led into a separate room.

After a super-boring movie about Jesus, we went to the chapel for devotions. The female lay director prayed, "Lord, I pray for all those here who need this retreat the most."

Well, that isn't me. I'm already a Christian. What I need is a hotel room.

Then she said, "And Lord, I pray for all those who think they need this retreat the least." I shivered as an invisible knife penetrated my cold heart.

We were then asked to remain silent until after communion the following morning.

No, no, no! When I'm in a new situation, I talk. That's how I cope.

I arrived at my room to find my roommate combing her hair. We hadn't yet met, and here I was with a vow of silence forced upon me.

"I don't like this not talking. What about you?" I queried.

"I'm not thrilled with it, but I'm willing to do it," she replied with a wide smile.

Ach! She's one of them.

We quickly exchanged names. "I'm so excited to be here," she said. Then she floated in her blissful bubble across the room and down the hall to the restrooms.

What have I gotten myself into?

The following day, the communion service was chock-full of responsive readings.

"The Lord is with you."

"And also with you."

"Lift up your hearts."

"We lift them up to the Lord."

Blah, blah, blah.

After the service, we were told to hug the people around us and say, "May the peace of Christ be with you." The other person was to respond with, "And also with you."

I stood stiff like a fallen icicle sticking straight up in a snowdrift. I didn't want people hugging me. I didn't know them; they didn't know me. Several people in the room also looked frozen, but many more were grinning from ear to ear.

And then, the woman on my left invaded my space and hugged me declaring, "May the peace of Christ be with you."

"Yeah, you, too," I mumbled.

The woman on my right, another smiling space invader, said, "Peace."

"Peace," I said in return.

Where had all these cheerful people come from? Did the leadership search under every rock in central Illinois for beaming faces? Did they put an ad in the newspaper? Wanted: happy people to intimidate unhappy people and make their lives even more miserable than they already are.

On Friday morning, we listened to two talks. The first was how God loved me before I was born. I knew this already, but I squirmed in my chair, wanting to go home.

I don't even love me right now.

The next talk was about how when a Christian encourages

or helps another person, it's really Christ, loving through the power of the Holy Spirit.

If that was true, I was in big trouble. The cold reception I gave the chapel huggers meant I had been chilly to Christ.

Thanks for the guilt trip. As if I wasn't feeling bad enough about myself already.

That evening back in our room, there were little notes of encouragement, scripture references, and candy on our pillows.

My roommate squealed, "Ohhh! Isn't this fun?"

When she left the room, I took the treats on my pillow and threw them, with force, into my suitcase in the closet. "Thanks, but no thanks!" I growled, slamming the door shut.

Saturday proved to be even more difficult. After each talk, I found my anger at Donn growing stronger. I hated how his job controlled my life. I knew he would want to volunteer on one of these retreats, which meant he would be gone even more often.

I resented looking out my kitchen window and seeing the church building staring back at me. I was tired of living in a house overseen by a committee. I was tired of being poor, tired of being nice, and tired of censoring every word that came out of my mouth. I wanted to swear like a sailor, dammit, whenever I damn well pleased!

During one of the talks, the speaker told us about the dying moments in her life. The times when she felt like her world had fallen apart, the times she felt all alone, and the times when memories of past hurts had crept back into her thoughts for her to relive all over again. She said, "In those times, God is always there wanting to comfort us, but we must allow Him in."

I fought hard to keep up my refrigeration, but it was starting to melt into tears. I desperately needed to cry.

The speaker said that the people who had spent months preparing the retreat were God's representatives to us. She said that hundreds of people worldwide were praying for us by name. Six people volunteering in the prayer chapel in the next room were also praying for each of us and praying for all thirteen speakers before, after, and during their talks.

I was emotionally touched that people who I didn't know were praying for me. The speaker said they were Jesus with skin. No wonder every time I felt the urge to pack my bags and sneak into town, I would feel an even stronger urge to stay and hear more.

A communion service followed the speech. As we took the bread and juice, we were to think of our dying moment and give it to God. My dying moment was the persistent loneliness in a ministry surrounded by Christians. Acknowledging this truth didn't take it away, but it felt lighter to carry.

At the closing service on Sunday afternoon, over two hundred people, our sponsors and past retreat attendees, were waiting for us. If willing, we could stand at the podium and share with the crowd what the weekend meant for us.

This was a serious moment for me. I wanted to be honest and spill my guts, but I was extremely nervous. I waited until almost everyone had spoken before heading to the podium. Looking at the crowd, I began my confession. "When I came here Thursday evening, I was very angry at Christians."

I swallowed, looked down at the podium, and briefly paused to collect my thoughts as the audience waited silently. Then I lifted my head and blurted, "I'm a minister's wife."

The room erupted in laughter.

What the...?

I wasn't trying to be funny. I was bearing my soul, admitting that three days earlier, I was a disgruntled miserable woman who came to the retreat with a secret plan to escape until she discovered she was stuck in the middle of nowhere. What happened to cause such a contradictory reaction? Was it my nervous hesitation before the reveal they found so amusing?

It took a while before the hilarity in the room settled down, which gave me time to compose myself before telling them how stressful the past year and a half had been and that the retreat helped me to work through some of my resentment toward Christians.

I returned home feeling less tied up in knots about my life, but that didn't change the "well-intentioned" dragons. I had to escape them, so I stepped down from choir director and switched churches, taking our children every Sunday to Donn's other church, where I was welcomed with open arms.

I taught the adult Sunday school class, creating my own curriculum to discuss the meaning of outdated lyrics we would sing during the church service that day, lyrics such as "he chastens and hastens" and "which wert and art and evermore shalt be." The class was unique and fun for the adults and helped my state of mind.

Leaving churches would eventually become routine for me.

Who Am I?

EVERY MORNING DONN GOT UP EARLY to spend time alone at the church. I admit I was jealous that God got that hour instead of me, but now that I felt more at peace and wasn't dissing His people as much as usual, I thought maybe I should spend time with Him, too.

The next day, I dragged myself out of bed at five-thirty in the morning to sit on the sofa my parents gave us when they moved to Florida. No more scratchy green couch for me! I opened the Bible, started reading, and promptly fell asleep. The following morning, the same thing happened.

This is not working!

The next morning, I gave it one more shot, but my head wouldn't stay above my shoulders. Then the strangest thing happened. I heard a voice say, "Go back to bed. Find out who you are, and then you'll know Me."

I was astonished. Did I really hear that? It wasn't something I would say. "Go back to bed," sure, but the other part? It sounded too profound to be from me.

I'd been struggling with my identity for a long time. I knew I was more than a wife, mother, and minister's spouse, but who was I? It was time to find out, especially now that I had permission to focus on myself.

I talked to Donn about helping with the kids in the morning. He said yes and offered to cut his God date short, get all three children up, and make breakfast so I could stay in bed. *Sweet!*

Sleeping a little longer and wandering downstairs to eat a cooked meal was a luxury, but I knew I needed more than extra sleep and breakfast to figure out who I was or wanted to be or whatever I was searching for.

I found a counseling center that took our insurance and scheduled an appointment for the following week. We had just purchased our first computer from Radio Shack: a TRS-80 Model 4 all-in-one with an attached keyboard. To expedite my first counseling session, I wrote the therapist a three-page typed letter, spilling my guts onto the page. Here are some highlights that aren't too personal to share.

- I try to please others to avoid conflict, but it doesn't always work.
- I've played make-believe minister's wife for so long that I don't know the real me.
- I've become bitter. I'm no fun. I'm way too serious. I don't like me anymore.
- I'm tired of putting everyone else first.
- I have no control or power over my own life!
- I feel like I'm going to crack at any moment.
- I've moved ten times in the past fourteen years. I want a home of my own.
- I feel like my husband's shadow.
- I don't want to be a minister's wife anymore.

During the visit, the counselor advised, "I think it would be helpful if you started journaling."

"Journaling? What's that?"

"It's writing your thoughts on paper daily, like the letter you wrote me."

She leaned forward in her chair with empathy in her eyes. "You've been carrying a heavy load for a long time. Suppressing your emotions isn't healthy."

My lower lip trembled. I'd finally found someone who could help me.

"You said in your letter that you felt better after writing, but there's a lot of unresolved anger to be released before you can get to what you really want to know, which is, who are you?"

"Will this be like an assignment I have to turn in? Are you going to read what I write?"

"Nope. It's for your eyes only. Get it all out. Swear as much as you want. Write whatever is on your mind. Think of it as a daily cleanse."

Putting my suppressed thoughts into solid form was the next best thing to breaking the "nice girl" rules I had created for myself.

The unexpressed anger exploded onto the page as I wrote about my life. The more I scribbled about those "well-intentioned" dragons, the more outlandish they became until they had personalities so outrageously embellished that I was rolling on the floor laughing at what I'd written.

None of the dragons were as awful as I had thought. My perception, though, through the eyes of anger and survival, had turned them into larger-than-life sitcom characters. And then it hit me. The girl who hates writing essays can write humor!

Who knew? Not me!

I never considered myself funny, but two hundred people had recently laughed at my words, and all I'd said was, "I'm a minister's wife." Maybe I am funny.

Now, what do I do with that insight?

A thought popped into my head that maybe I could write short stories about being a minister's wife. I would call it *The Secret Life of the Minister's Wife*. My readers would laugh at my anecdotes while learning that clergy wives are ordinary people.

My next thought was, "I need to take a creative writing class!"

We'd bought Donn a new car a year earlier, so the red station wagon was now mine. I buckled Karen into her car seat and hightailed it to the community college fifteen miles away to get a course catalog. A creative writing class was scheduled for the spring semester, just a few months away.

Donn was hesitant when I told him I wanted to return to college. He later admitted he was scared I would meet someone else and fall in love. At the time, I thought his fear was ridiculous. Our marriage had its issues, as all marriages do, but I couldn't exist in the world alone with three children and no job. And besides, marriage is for life, right?

My biggest issue was that Karen was only three and a half years old. What would I do with her during the day if Donn had a church emergency and couldn't watch her? And then, another thought popped into my head. Maybe I could do the class as an independent study course?

Wow! Where did that idea come from?

My request was approved after speaking with the instructor. I would send my stories and poems to her via the post office every week, and she would respond with her comments. I earned an A grade and another three hours of credit toward my college degree.

Woo-hoo!

Donn had requested a new church from the conference, and in April, we were notified we would move in June. I was ready to go, but that meant leaving a good friend behind. She was older than me and the only church member I trusted to talk about the well-intentioned dragons. Right before we left, she gave me a going-away card.

There's an ancient Indian custom that says when two friends are about to leave each other, they wrap their bodies in bark and then float down the river side by side and talk about old times. Let's not do that.

Although the past three years were emotionally painful, they forced me to be honest about what I did and didn't want. In the following five years, I would emerge from my self-made cocoon, open my wings, and learn to fly.

Concord/Arenzville

1986 to 1991

IN JUNE 1986, A MONTH AFTER my class ended, we moved to another two-point charge in the same district as when we lived in Perry.

The house in Concord (population 205) was across the street from a large Methodist church that housed a small congregation and a few children. The other church, in Arenzville (population 500), was four miles north. Their building was medium-sized, with many young adults, a slew of children, and an after-school program called God's Kids.

Both churches were in rural farming communities that raised pigs and planted corn and soybeans. Thankfully, there were no well-intentioned dragons in either church, but there were more house problems.

As you know, I have issues living in houses owned by other people. My dad was a builder. When Mom wanted a larger kitchen, Dad built it for her. When Melody wanted her own bedroom, he built a fourth bedroom in the basement and added a recreation room for the whole family to enjoy, complete with a pool table that Julie spent so much time playing she couldn't be defeated.

In the ministry, we didn't have a landlord; we had a committee of church members who decided what we could and couldn't do to the house. When we moved to Concord, I already resented waiting for others to determine if I could have a shower on the main level, a bedroom with heat, or new carpet. I had become David, fighting the giant Goliath with an empty slingshot and nothing more than a tube of lipstick to hurl.

The house was a one-and-a-half-story American bungalow. The upstairs was a livable attic with sloped walls, hence the half story. It had one bedroom with a door and wide floor planks that took up one-third of the space. The other two-thirds was a generous open space with a 1970s long shag carpet in an ugly mixture of faded greens and yellows that constantly got wrapped around the brush rollers of my Electrolux vacuum. The second-hand carpeting donated by a church member who no longer wanted it was laid on the plank floor without a pad underneath. At least the space had heat, unlike the bedrooms of our first house!

The main level had two bedrooms. At the front of the house, our bedroom had one small closet that was only as deep as a metal hanger. It was five feet wide inside, yet we could only access two and a half feet of clothing because the small door wasn't in the middle of the closet.

To remedy the lack of closet space, the church had closed in the front porch, added eight thin storm windows but no regular windows, and added two supersized closets one on each end of the front porch. What the space didn't have was heat!

Donn and I hung our clothes in one of those closets. At first, it was manageable until winter rolled around. The average low temperature in central Illinois in January is nineteen degrees Fahrenheit. In the morning, I put on the clothes I'd worn the day before, adding my winter coat, hat, scarf, socks, and shoes to get clothes for the day out of our front porch "freezer."

What is up with these houses and no heat?

The church knew a closet on the front porch wasn't a good solution, but they couldn't agree on a plan to correct it. I awoke one night with detailed plans for extending the house onto the front porch. The blueprint included a good-sized closet in our bedroom, another in the living room for games, blankets, etc., and one in the foyer with a low bar so the children could reach their coats.

The parsonage committee liked my design and eventually used it to remodel the house while we still lived there. This remodeling job came up in conversation when I was co-chair of a central Illinois ministers' wives retreat. I wrote the following poem to promote the event.

Fall Retreat

Although our faces shine so sweet,
and some say we are the elite,
ofttimes we feel incomplete.
Do I belong? Am I obsolete?
What we need is a fall retreat.
Remove our masks. Put up our feet.
Where other wives we can meet
whose lives, like ours, are bittersweet.
And so to you, I do entreat.
Come to the fall wives' retreat!
Sing. Play games. Share and eat!
Go home calm and replete.

At the retreat, I passed a group of women talking about parsonages and overheard our district superintendent's wife say, "We had two houses in our district that needed updating. One needed a new kitchen, and the other needed closet space. It took years, but the churches finally got it done."

Then she pointed at me, saying, "And Gaye lived in both houses when they remodeled."

"You're welcome," I said with a curtsy.

At this point, Donn had pastored eleven churches, and we had lived in five church-owned houses. Since then, our first parsonage was torn down, the one with the new kitchen burned down, and the other three have been sold.

These retreats were the only places where clergy wives could talk honestly. When someone said "parsonage beige" we all knew it meant the paint in parsonages that would go with every new minister's furniture. The retreat was a place to connect with the only people who truly understood the loneliness and frustration of being a minister's wife.

A female guest minister was invited to speak at one of our retreats. She ended her talk with a prayer to Mother/Father God. *What?*

Her language didn't resonate with me, but I could see the logic after thinking about it. Why couldn't God be female? More likely, God was neither male nor female. I mean, why would a spirit need reproductive parts?

In my quest to discover who I was so I could understand who God is, I began reading self-help books. The first one was *The Cinderella Complex: Women's Hidden Fear of Independence* by Colette Dowling. It's about women's fear of independence, which leads them to believe they must be rescued by a male, preferably a handsome Prince Charming on a white stallion.

When I was growing up in the fifties, only 34 percent of the women in the United States worked outside the home. By the end of the sixties, that number had jumped to 37 percent, yet a woman's identity was still homemaker, wife, and mother.

While we sat in front of the television watching *Father Knows Best* and *The Beverly Hillbillies*, TV commercials taught us how to be the perfect wife and mother. The unexpected side effect was that it also trained us to fear the opinions of others.

What will people think if...

- My windows and floors don't sparkle?
- My family's clothes aren't the brightest of the bright?
- My husband's shirts have that dreaded ring around the collar?

Society didn't encourage females to think of themselves as independent. I had no idea how to deal with conflict other than avoiding it like the plague.

By the end of the seventies, women made up 43 percent of the workforce, yet advertising still ingrained within me the concept that, as a woman, I was responsible for the happiness of everyone around me.

Even Christianity promoted this concept: Jesus first. Others second. Yourself last. I went into marriage believing that if I sacrificed what I desired for what my spouse wanted, the sacrifice and love would be reciprocated. When that didn't happen, I blamed Donn and the Church. I carried none of the blame, or so I thought.

I'm innocent, your Honor!

By the end of the eighties, the number of women in the workforce had jumped to 57 percent. TV ads were now telling us that we could work outside the home *and* fulfill our responsibilities at home. An excellent example of this is the iconic commercial slogan: "Enjoli, the eight-hour perfume for the twenty-four-hour woman."

The jingle for this 1982 Enjoli commercial goes like this:

'Cause I'm a woman,
I can bring home the bacon, fry it up in a pan,
and never, ever let you forget you're a man!
I can work till five o'clock,
come home and read you Tickety Tock,
and if it's lovin' you want, I can kiss you and give you the shivers.

The 1979 version was:

I can put the wash on the line, feed the kids, get dressed,
pass out the kisses, and get to work by five of nine cause I'm a
woman.
I can bring home the bacon, fry it up in a pan,
and never, ever let you forget you're a man!

(Both ads are available on YouTube.)

It wasn't until I read *Women Who Love Too Much: When You Keep Wishing and Hoping He'll Change* by Robin Norwood that I accepted responsibility for my role in the marriage.

How could I expect Donn to know how I felt if I repeatedly pretended everything was okay? I held my tongue more often than not. If I did speak and Donn disagreed, I deferred to him because the Bible said he was the head of the house.

I decided right then that this "man of the house" idea was hogwash. It was written thousands of years ago by men. It doesn't apply in this day and age because women are no longer considered property. Marriage is a partnership, with no one person in charge.

The Dance of Anger: A Woman's Guide to Changing the Patterns of Intimate Relationships by Harriet Goldhor Lerner, PhD, was the next book on my to-read list.

When couples, family members, or coworkers are angry with each other, they respond the same way every time. It's like a familiar partner dance routine where one of the partners tries to convince the other partner to change their dance steps while unwilling to change their own.

Another big takeaway for me was that I can't change anyone. I can only change myself. If I want the dance to change, I have to change my reaction to the conflict by using non-threatening statements and taking responsibility for my feelings. My partner then has the option to dance with me or not.

Sometimes I still step back into those old familiar dance routines, but what has stuck with me all these years is that if I want something to change, the responsibility to make it happen is all mine.

If you want to discover what's keeping you from living the life you want, self-help books are the next best thing to professional counseling and are way less expensive.

Knowledge is power. Every book I read gave me more courage to stop hiding behind my plastic smile.

Octopus Day Care

THE DREAM WAS THE SAME ONE I'd been having for several months. My high school band room is filled with voices and the click-clack sound of opening and closing instrument cases as we prepare for rehearsal.

My used clarinet is pungent as usual, with forty years of cork grease embedded in the velvet lining of the case in which it's stored. The smell will stay with me until I wash my hands after class.

"I thought you dropped out of the band," Sharon, a fellow clarinet player, asks. "You haven't been here all semester."

Shocked, I reply, "I haven't?"

I'm going to college next year to get a music degree. Why didn't I sign up for the band?

The heat of embarrassment rises on my neck when the scene suddenly shifts from the music room to the school gymnasium. It's boys' basketball season. Both teams are warming up on the court. Basketballs fly through the air with a swish or a thunk when they hit the hoop's rim.

I'm on the sidelines in my Harvard Hornets gold and black cheerleading uniform, white ankle socks, and white Keds, ready to head out onto the court for the school song with my cheering squad.

I take my place on the floor with the other four girls, Chris, Alice, Charlotte, and Sharon, the clarinetist. The pep band plays the school song intro, and we begin the routine. "Come, cheer for Harvard, for H. C. H. S, for old gold and black o'er head..."

Wait, something's wrong. I'm doing the same routine we've used for the past three years, but the girls are doing something new—a lump forms in my throat. I don't remember the last time I practiced with the team.

Did I drop out of cheerleading, too? Why am I here?

My legs are heavy as I leave the court to grab my coat from my locker in the hallway right outside the gymnasium door.

Why is it so difficult to move?

Looking down, I find my three children wrapped around my legs. With a sigh of relief, it dawns on me. I graduated from high school fifteen years ago. I'm married with children. I'm not supposed to be here.

Upon awakening, I realized the nightmare was not about high school but my unfinished college degree.

That afternoon, with the vision still fresh in my mind, I sat on the back porch steps of the parsonage with a shawl of discouragement weighing down my shoulders.

As quickly as the tears came, a stronger, more powerful thought replaced them. At the first Walk to Emmaus retreat, where I disliked all Christians except the older couple next door, one of the speakers said, "It's okay to sit on the pity potty, but don't stay there too long or all you'll get is a red ring."

I immediately dried my tears and told myself, "If you want to return to college, make it happen! Prince Charming isn't going to ride in on a white horse with a college acceptance letter for you."

I registered at McMurray College, thirteen miles away in Jacksonville, and received a vocal music scholarship. I found day care for Karen in a Baptist church near the college. I didn't have time to check it out first, but I trusted it would be a loving place, like Mr. Rogers' Neighborhood.

Karen, now four years old, had never been to day care. When she realized I was leaving her that first day, she wrapped her legs around my waist and her arms around my neck in a python-like grip and let out blood-curdling screams. The more I tried to release her octopus-like suction-cupped limbs, the louder she screamed.

The two adults in the room stared at me as I struggled to pry the sea creature off my body. Frustrated, I raised my voice, "Would someone please help me?"

An older woman who sat calmly in a chair watching me wrestle the little octopus sighed and stood up and, like molasses, slowly made her way to where I stood.

Hurry up, lady! I have to get to class!

She couldn't get Karen released either. Another woman wandered over. Were they both on drugs or just tired? Between the two, they managed to unwind my daughter's octopus appendages.

Karen's anguished wailing haunted me as I rushed to my car and cried during the two-minute drive to campus, wiping her tears and mine off my cheeks and neck before heading to my first class.

This better be worth it!

A music degree requires more classes per semester than a typical degree, as the classes are worth fewer credit hours. For example, English, math, and science courses are worth three or four credit hours, but in music, required classes like band, choir, voice, and instrument lessons are worth only half a credit.

As a music major, I had to pick a band instrument to learn.

Since I registered late, all the instruments had been spoken for except the trombone, which was awkward to carry and even more awkward to play. I wasn't fond of it at all.

I could have practiced at the college but didn't have the time. Concert choir ran from 5:00 to 6:00 p.m. four days a week, and the day care closed at five-thirty. After my last class at 2:50 p.m., with books in one arm and the trombone in another, I hiked to the car, drove to the day care, picked up Karen, rushed home to get supper started, then headed back into town for concert choir.

By the time I got home at six-thirty, the meal I had prepared, which typically fed our family of five, had been gobbled up by the four. I quickly ate a bowl of soup, practiced the trombone, which no one in the house appreciated, and did homework until midnight.

I didn't make more food for supper because we were still a low-income family. Our children received reduced meals at school, but we still had to be frugal about everything we bought. I didn't buy ice cream, cookies, chips, or soda because they weren't necessities.

Once when returning from the grocery store, Karen overheard me telling Donn, "I only bought the bare necessities."

A few moments later, standing on a kitchen chair, Karen started digging through the grocery sacks.

"What are you looking for, sweetheart?" I asked.

She put her hands on her hips and, with a puzzled expression, said, "I can't find that new stuff you bought—bare necessities."

The following four college days were exact repeats, from the octopus to plates licked clean at home. By the weekend, Karen and I had strep throat. I was underfed and exhausted mentally, emotionally, and physically.

On Monday, I returned the trombone and dropped out of school—again. It wasn't a sacrifice on my part. I considered my family, but I did it primarily for me. That week of college opened my eyes to three truths:

- I don't need a degree to teach music. I'd given voice lessons, directed two choirs, led the singing in Sunday school and Bible school, and played piano for church. I was still doing most of these musical activities, and Donn and I were still performing here and there.
- The voice I heard while rocking Karen when we lived in Perry was accurate. I would never be a public school music teacher, and I was more than okay with that.
- If I ever return to college, I will choose a degree with three- and four-credit hour classes. No more dragging a trombone around, dumping my daughter with strangers, or leaving my family during dinner for half a credit.

My decision to stay home for a few more years until Karen was in school turned out to be a wise choice of action.

When the volunteer organist at the church quit in 1987, Donn asked me to take her place. I'd never played the organ, but I had watched my mother do it. Surely I could figure it out. So every day for several weeks, Karen accompanied me to the church, sitting at my side, just as I did with my mom, as I trained my hands, feet, and eyes to work independently.

CHAPTER 19

Well, Knock Me Over!

THAT SAME YEAR, I WAS ASKED to participate in another Walk to Emmaus retreat as a member of the prayer chapel. This would make it my third time attending and my second time serving on a team.

Along with five other women on the prayer team, our responsibilities were to lay hands on and pray for every speaker before and after they spoke. During their talk, we prayed for each attendee by name.

Doris, one of my teammates, had a most unusual way of praying. She'd say, "I see you wearing a yellow raincoat. On your head is a matching rain hat, and on your feet are yellow galoshes. You are completely protected from doubts and fears about speaking, for they land on your rain gear and slide right off."

I was fascinated by this fun, memorable, and quick new way of praying. If every minister painted a picture with their prayers instead of droning on repeatedly with flowery words that no one remembers afterward, think how powerfully unforgettable that would be for the congregation! It would certainly help me, for when I close my eyes while someone prattles on my behalf, my mind automatically jumps at the opportunity to wander off freely.

I thoroughly enjoyed this three-day behind-the-scenes ministry. On Sunday afternoon, a few hours before the retreat ended, Nancy, one of the assistant lay leaders, wandered into the prayer chapel, asking to be anointed to overcome being intimidated by other people. Martin, an assistant spiritual leader for the event, was in the chapel and suggested that Nancy kneel so we could lay hands on her. The rest of us gathered around her, shoulder to shoulder, when Martin asked, "Does anyone else want to be anointed to overcome the intimidation of others?"

Doris, who was standing next to me, kneeled next to Nancy. My heart began to pound. The urge to join them was immediate and powerful. It consumed me, but as usual, I hesitated. It wasn't like that first Jesus rally when I didn't respond due to what the church members might think. This time, it was a crisis of word choice. Did I need to overcome the "intimidation" of others, or was my issue the "fear" of what others might think? I didn't want to be anointed for the wrong thing.

Time is running out, Gaye; make up your mind!

Suddenly, something plowed into the back of my knees and I dropped to the floor right next to Doris.

What was that?

I didn't hear a word Martin was saying. I was fixated on how I ended up on my knees and the heat radiating throughout my neck, shoulders, and upper back as if someone had laid a heating pad on me and turned the setting up to hot. When the anointing ended, everyone stepped away as Doris and Nancy stood up, but I was frozen.

When I finally lifted my head, Martin was staring at me. With a soft voice, he said, "Something has happened to you. I can see it in your face."

Something happened alright, but what? No one had been behind me. I can only describe it as a super powerful blast of wind on the back of my knees. Maybe it was the *Star Wars* Force.

As I explained what happened, I had no idea if anyone believed me, but I didn't care. That in itself was out of the ordinary. Logic insisted that a strong wind inside a closed room was not scientifically possible, especially since I was the only one who felt it. Even so, something invisible knocked me forward, and my upper body was still radiating heat.

During the next break, I headed to my room feeling calm and confident, like I was inside a bubble of serenity.

Could this be that same bubble on which my first retreat room-mate floated?

When I returned to the chapel, I joined the group in prayer for a female minister attending her first retreat. She was holed up in her room, refusing to participate. Ah, yes, the first-time resistance. I remember it well.

As we prayed for her, I knew that Donn was the one to talk to her. He wasn't on the team, but I knew he would be coming for the closing event and would be there soon. I listened to my intuition, left the prayer room, and saw him walking down the hall toward me.

We hadn't seen each other since I left the house on Thursday. I went up to him, and with authority neither of us had ever seen me use, I told him about the struggling minister. "You need to talk to her. Come with me," I commanded.

I took Donn to her room, knocked on the door, introduced them, and left. I learned later that she rejoined the group and finished the retreat. Afterward, she found me and said, "Thank you. I needed to talk to a minister who wasn't part of the weekend."

Wow! My intuition was correct!

The heat on my neck and shoulders lasted over a week. When I discovered that my neighbor, a cranky older man who lived across the street, was in the hospital, I felt the impulse to visit him.

He wasn't much of a talker, but we visited as best we could. Then, without intimidation, I asked if he would allow me to pray for him. I stood at the end of his bed, put my hands on his blanket where his feet were, and prayed aloud using a visual he could remember. As I left the hospital, I was amazed that this newfound boldness was manifesting in my everyday life. Overcoming intimidation must have been my issue, after all.

The only explanation for my experience was that the Holy Spirit/Force had touched me. I knew God loved me unconditionally. Jesus was my best friend who listened to my woes and never spread them around town. But the Holy Spirit/Force physically knocked me to my knees when I was stuck in my own head.

We all need a friend who loves and listens, but we also need one who will push us off the high-diving board when we are scared to jump.

I bought a newly published book about the power of the Holy Spirit. I don't remember the title, but when Donn saw it, he was concerned and told me I shouldn't read it. I ignored him.

The rebel preacher doesn't want me to read a book about the Holy Spirit? What's up with that?

After the prayer chapel event, I realized I did have my own ministry. My involvement in teaching Sunday school to children and adults for fifteen years opened up a creative side I didn't know I had. I loved finding innovative, fun ways to teach. I was more than just a wife, mother, and singer. I was a teacher. *Surprise!*

Then one morning, Donn announced that he had talked to God about becoming a missionary. I knew he was dismayed with local church ministry, but the mission field?

"You mean like our whole family moving to Africa?"

"Yes."

OVER MY DEAD BODY!

I didn't say that out loud because I'd been through something similar in 1974 when Donn came home with an electric piano for our music ministry that we couldn't afford and didn't need. Every day, I visualized that piano leaving our apartment. Five days later, it was returned without me saying a word.

Although I was reading books about standing up for myself, I still couldn't do it on demand. So, I used that same electric piano technique for the missionary thing by keeping my mouth shut and imagining the idea fading out of Donn's head, but it didn't fade away. He had already contacted several missionary organizations, and the Baptists sent two applications, one for him and one for me! *Yikes!*

A few months earlier, a missionary couple spoke at our church. The man did all the talking about "their" ministry. When I asked his wife what she did on the mission field, she said, "I invite the local women to my house for tea and conversation one day a week."

She left the U.S. to be a missionary overseas, and her job was tea parties? No, thank you.

I still believed that the mission field would never happen. Even so, I wrote my application honestly, explaining that I wouldn't leave the United States and wanted to be a full-fledged missionary, not just the wife of one.

Two weeks later, Donn received a letter denying his application because, I quote, "Your wife has issues." It wasn't my "issues" that kept my family out of the mission field. It was my honesty.

✳✳✳

Karen began kindergarten right after the "knockdown" retreat. Back then, kindergarten was half a day. Having time alone in the house was priceless.

One day in early December, when Karen was at school, I thought about all the open houses and parsonage issues I'd dealt with and got myself into a snit. Why couldn't I let these things go? So, I journaled about it.

Before I even sat down to write, a poem was forming. It was a combination of all the parsonages I'd lived in plus a heap of exaggeration. Here is "Twas the Night before Open House."

Twas the night before open house
at the minister's abode.
The house needed updates.
Church members were told.
The curtains still hung
twenty years on the wall.
The carpet lay bare
where it ran down the hall.
The children shivered
and shook in the cold,
for the windows were cracked
and the furnace was old.
With preacher in long johns
and me in pink flannel,
we turned on the TV
and just changed the channel.

When up from the basement
we heard a commotion.
We sprang from the sofa
and set right in motion.
Away to the basement
we ran in our fright,
threw open the door
and flipped on the light.
And what to our eyes
did we then behold?
A moving blob
of slimy green mold.
It crawled in the washer.
It crept up the dryer.
It rolled by the furnace,
growing wider and higher.
It raced to the stairsteps
as if it was lightning.
We bolted the door;
it was so frightening.
Then into the kitchen,
right under the door,
it slipped in the house
and slimed the floor.
It slid through each room
as if it could see,
leaving the house
with gooey debris.
Then up on the table
it crept like a louse,
devouring the cookies

for my open house.
With hunger subsided
it rested all night
and still hadn't moved
with morning's first light.
We slept on the counter
and stayed there all day
'til the church folk arrived,
their visit to pay.
"You can't live like this!"
they exclaimed one and all.
We'll build a new house,
and this time we won't stall.
So into a new home
my family settled.
And I paid the slime man
for wares he had peddled.

A month later, I saw an ad for a writer's group called Jacksonville Area Writers that met once a month.

What perfect timing! This is just what I need.

I attended my first meeting, having no idea that members brought a story, article, or poem they wrote to read, and then the group leader collected them and dropped them off at the local newspaper for publication.

I wanted, more than anything, to tell people through humor what it was like to be a minister's wife, but that was a *future* goal, not *today's* goal. I tentatively lifted a hand. "Excuse me. This is a requirement?"

The leader smiled. "Yes, it forces us to write something every month that we know will be read by others."

"I write short stories about being a minister's wife. I'm not ready for the parishioners to know I'm the author."

"That's no problem; use a pen name."

I became a published writer a few days after the next meeting. It was a bit embarrassing that every month the newspaper published my stories first, but I was the only member who wrote humor, and the paper liked fun stories.

Five months later, a member of the Arenzville congregation stopped me in the church foyer.

"Have you been reading those stories in the newspaper by that minister's wife?"

Uh oh. Does she suspect it's me?

I cautiously replied, "Yes, I have."

It wasn't a lie. I always read them after they were published.

"Well," she began.

Okay, here it comes. She knows.

"I think the two of you would get along great!"

I burst out laughing. "You know, I think we would, too."

Over the next year, I published twelve minister's wife stories in the newspaper and two in a minister's spouse publication called *Spice*, plus two articles in the newspaper, five in two different Sunday school magazines, and two in the conference newsletter. I only used a pen name for the minister's wife's stories in the newspaper.

The poem "Twas the Night before Open House" was published the following December. I added the following disclaimer to my bio just in case someone from the church found out I was the author: *Ellen Richards (pen name) is an overimaginative minister's wife and a member of Jacksonville Area Writers. The above poem was written in jest and is in no way a reflection of her current living condition.*

Blindfolds and Warm Maple Syrup

IT WAS 1988. I WAS THIRTY-FOUR; my children were thirteen, ten, and six. Karen was now in first grade. I had every school day by myself to write and was getting published but only got paid in copies. I sent my minister's wife's stories to both secular and religious magazines, but according to the rejection letters, they "weren't a good fit." My take was they were too religious for the mainstream magazines and too honest, open, and revealing for religious magazines.

I seriously considered getting a job in Jacksonville. Still, I wasn't interested in the Enjoli stress of bringing home the bacon, frying it up in a pan, and making sure my husband didn't forget he was a man. A woman can only do so much after working all day. Plus, we were in marriage counseling, which wasn't going well.

A day or two later, I answered a knock on my front door. Jim, the owner of the feed store next to our house, stood outside. "Hey Gaye, I was wondering if you'd be interested in working a couple of hours three days a week preparing invoices for my customers."

Yes! "I'd love to, Jim."

The band/cheerleading dream returned in the spring of 1989. It was the same as before, from the smell of the clarinet to the cheerleading uniform and children wrapped around my legs. It was time for me to return to college, this time for an English degree.

Fifty miles away in Springfield was Sangamon State University (SSU), a nontraditional junior/senior college founded eighteen years earlier in 1971 for adult learners. All my previous college credits would transfer.

Classes were taught day and night, four days a week. Each class met twice a week for one and a half hours each day or one evening a week for three hours. According to the catalog, I could arrange my schedule to attend only on Tuesdays and Thursdays.

I would have three days of quiet time at home to study while the kids were in school, plus I could keep my job at the feed store by working it around my school schedule. The only problem was that I needed one science class to qualify for admission.

So, I attended Illinois College in Jacksonville for one semester in the fall. I applied for and received a Federal Pell Grant, which paid for all my classes and books. So instead of just a science class, I tacked on sociology, writing, and literature.

In biology, the most demanding class, I achieved 100 percent on every exam, including the final. This was a phenomenal accomplishment for a girl who once thought her friends were smarter than she was. I earned thirteen credit hours with a 4.00 grade point average for the semester.

I'm a straight-A student! Woo-hoo!

I transferred to SSU for the spring semester of 1990. All my courses were worth four hours of credit. Donn was very supportive, taking over all the laundry duties, getting the children up for school, and cooking all the meals when I was gone from morning to late evening.

One semester, I had a class on Tuesday evening followed by an early Wednesday morning class and spent the night in Springfield at my in-laws'. I couldn't have finished my degree without Donn's help.

Going back to college was an excellent excuse to get out of playing the organ at Concord and start attending the Arenzville church, where there were more people to teach Sunday school, and I wouldn't be expected to do anything. *Yay!*

One of my first classes was called Credit for Prior Learning, which means knowledge acquired from regular life: work, independent study, volunteering, community service, etc. The course, held on five Saturdays throughout the semester, taught me how to write a portfolio about my past learning experiences, which would translate into college credit through writing essays and gathering documentation to prove I did what I said I did.

The educational goal statement, autobiography, and chronological record of my life from 1971 through 1990 were written during the course. Over the summer, I wrote the essays, assembled the documents, and submitted the portfolio the first week of the fall semester.

I received four hours for the Saturday course and another sixteen hours the following semester when my portfolio was assessed for Music Performance, Writing for Publication, Communication with the Deaf, and Experiential Learning with Elementary Students, which was based on my years teaching Sunday school and the week-long Bible school I ran using learning centers.

With those sixteen hours, plus the sixteen hours of credit from my regular classes, I earned two semesters in one. Only one more semester left to finish my degree! *Yippie!*

The one vivid memory I have of this course was when the instructor shared that tarot cards were a tool she used for guidance.

Tarot cards? Aren't they evil?

I look back at my reaction now and wonder why I could readily accept that Edgar Cayce could be a Christian and a psychic yet turn my nose down at someone who used tarot cards, especially since, at the time, I knew nothing about them.

My favorite teacher was Jacqueline Jackson, an accomplished novelist and published writer of children's books. In her perceptual writing course, she created activities to invite story ideas from our senses and experiences. We went people-watching at the mall and to the Girl Scout camp to sit at the beach for an hour without speaking. We had a day to taste food and one for smelling scents we each brought to class on cotton balls. We could write about the experience or anything the encounter brought up for us.

On a warm September day, I got to class early. Jackie handed me a scarf and told me to pick a partner for a blind trust walk. Most of the students hadn't arrived yet, which left me to choose one of three girls in their twenties or a man my age. I was a lonely married woman. Why wander around campus with a girl when I could be with a man?

Ron's blue eyes lit up when I handed him the scarf. This writing exercise would be much more fun than smelling cotton balls and tasting food.

I knew Ron worked on campus, although I didn't know which department. He came to class every week wearing blue jeans and a perfectly pressed button-down-the-front, short-sleeved cotton shirt of various plaid or checked colors. Clean-shaven, with light brown hair, Ron walked confidently, making his six-foot height appear even taller. I surmised he had a military background.

"Jackie said we could go anywhere on campus. How about outside?" Ron suggested.

Yawning and rolling my shoulders to get out the kinks, I said, "That sounds great! I've been inside all day."

"Ladies first," he said, swishing the scarf in his hand toward the stairs.

When we stepped outside, I turned my back to him. He tied the scarf over my eyes, wrapped his bare arm in my bare arm, and began leading me around.

"Have you ever been to the pond?" he inquired.

"No, I haven't."

It was just a body of water near where I parked my car. I was a woman on a mission to get my degree. Investigating a small lagoon was not a priority, but I was here now, and Ron would tell me all about what I had been missing.

Blindfolded, I focused on his low smooth bass clarinet voice. It warmed me like warm maple syrup. *Yum!* He spoke slowly, with pauses between sentences, which helped me visualize his words. "The pond is oval, about the size of two hot air balloons. Lily pads are lazing on the water's surface near where you're standing. Can you see them in your mind?"

Oh yeah...

"The water's very still right now, like glass. On the east, to your right, there's brown moss. Most people look at it and think it's pond scum, but it's not. About five feet in front of you, fish are just beneath the surface. I can see their tiny air bubbles breaking the water into small circles. Oh! Did you hear that? A baby frog leaped out of the water onto a concrete slab."

He took the palm of my hand, drawing a circle to show me the size of the little frog. If I had explored the pond by myself, I would have missed the beauty of his perspective—and that gorgeous voice. He sure had a way with words. And, good golly, he smelled good, too.

When I blindfolded him and took his arm in mine, he put his other hand on my arm. I led him toward the Brookens Library, trying to give him the detailed experience he had given me, and then, he gently caressed my arm. It felt nice.

I didn't stop him until a few minutes later when my conscience yelled, "What are you doing, Gaye?"

I turned to Ron and asked, "What are you doing?"

Ron quickly released his hand. "I apologize. Your skin is very soft, and this is a blind sensory exercise, right?"

I chuckled at his comeback and said, "It's okay." *I wasn't lying.*

We saw each other in class and occasionally said hello, but he was just one of many guys in my writing class.

College was a ball. I was thirty-eight years old, with friends who knew me as another adult student finishing a degree rather than a minister's wife. I was no longer the naïve eighteen-year-old who slipped and fell onto another person's life path. I was growing by leaps and bounds, soaking up every bit of information that came my way. The big question was, what would I do with this new me?

There's a Storm Brewing

WEDNESDAY, MARCH 27, 1991, WAS BLUSTERY. The flat central Illinois prairie tends to be breezy most days, with an average wind speed in March of nine miles per hour. On this day, the wind was strong, coming from the southwest at twenty-five miles per hour.

As I drove east toward Springfield on Interstate 72, using both hands on the steering wheel and paying attention, I had no problem keeping the car on the road and arrived at the university in record time with the wind's assistance.

After my morning class, I ate a ham sandwich and Fritos and drank a Pepsi, then headed to the fourth floor of Brookens Library to study in my favorite spot near the large windows on the east side of the building as I waited for my evening class.

As the afternoon progressed, the wind picked up. By four o'clock, the library windows were rattling. I picked up my books, heading to the lower level for safety, when an announcement came over the loudspeaker: "Your attention, please! Sangamon State will be closing at five o'clock today due to dangerous winds. All evening classes are canceled."

The announcement was repeated as I took the stairs with other students to the main level and out the door to the northeast parking lot by the pond. With books clutched in front of me and the wind pushing me from behind, I arched my back, walking with my feet spread apart to keep from falling forward. From far away, I probably looked like a waddling pregnant woman.

The wind was now at seventy-one miles per hour. Gripping the steering wheel as I headed west, I could feel the tension in my elbows as I struggled to keep the car on the interstate while dodging flying debris.

I was shaking when I pulled the car into my parking spot next to our one-car garage. The storm had been a lot to deal with, but another storm was waiting for me on the horizon that I hadn't had time to process.

Donn had decided to leave local church ministry, which meant we would have to move out of our house in June after my graduation. He applied for several jobs in the chaplaincy field but had not yet been called for an interview.

Having no idea where we would be living, I couldn't start job hunting. What if Donn didn't find a job come moving day? Where would we go? What would we do with both of us unemployed and three children to support?

The following Sunday, March 31, sitting in the Arenzville church with the kids, I noticed the front of the church bulletin depicted a descending dove with the words: *The Holy Spirit will lead you into all Truth.*

With light shining through the stained-glass windows onto the bulletin in my hand, I knew the truth—I would never be happy in this marriage. From the first day sitting by myself in church next to the "you're in my seat" lady instead of on a honeymoon, I should have known we never had a chance. My mother knew it. I suspected it and was determined to make it work, but I was done trying now.

Like Tom Hanks in the movie *Big* and Jennifer Garner in *13 Going on 30*, we woke up the day after our wedding and had become grownups pretending we knew what we were doing.

We had many good times, especially when we sang together and when the kids came, adding a bounty of love and entertainment. But our marriage was a loose-knit sweater in a constant state of getting snagged and coming apart. We didn't have the time or the energy to focus on repairs while putting Jesus first, others second, and our marriage last.

Due to the windstorm and the cancellation of my Wednesday evening class the week before, the following day, Monday, April 1, I went to the fourth floor of the Public Affairs Center building (PAC) after lunch instead of the library to ask the professor what syllabus topic we would be talking about that week.

It wasn't like this information was vital, but it seemed extremely important to me then, so much so that I changed my routine, only to discover the professor wasn't in his office. The PAC is a four-story octagon-shaped building that houses the Sangamon Auditorium, cafeteria, classrooms, faculty offices, and an atrium on the third floor in the middle of the building.

As I looked down at the atrium from the fourth-floor walkway, I had an impulse to study on one of the inviting sofas rather than a cubical in the library. I took the elevator down one floor and settled on a cozy couch to read *Pet Cemetery* by Stephen King for a class called "Aspects of Popular Culture" when my blind trust walk partner, Ron, wandered through.

He wore his typical blue jeans and a plaid cotton shirt. This time it was shades of green and long sleeves. I hadn't seen him since last semester, but I had overheard a classmate say that Ron was in Guam for two weeks' active duty with the Navy. I was right about his military training.

"Hi!" His face beamed when my voice caught his attention. "Gaye! It's great to see you."

Taking a seat in the chair butted up next to the sofa I sat on, he took my hand, lacing his fingers with mine, and said, "How have you been? Have you written anything lately? What are you reading? Ah! Stephen King! That's a good one."

I took great pleasure in that voice, his focused attention on me, and the touch of his hand in mine. He held on for at least two minutes. Sensations that had laid dormant for years erupted within me as my hand soaked up his warmth. The feeling wasn't sexual. It was more like seeing a good friend after a long parting. I didn't have a reaction like this when we were arm in arm during the blind trust walk. Well, maybe when he spoke with that sexy low voice.

What's going on with me?

Loneliness echoed in my head. "You've been starving for affection, approval, and encouragement for a long time."

You're right! My touch quota has been way down.

At Ron's invitation, I followed him to his office, a one-person copy center to serve the west end of campus just around the corner from the atrium. After four years in the Navy, he joined the Navy Reserve and used the GI Bill to complete an associate's degree. He chose the printing field because he was an avid reader. What better place to read academic papers than in a university print shop? As an employee, he took classes for free and was close to finishing a degree in communications.

After thirty minutes, Logic said, "You should leave."

Loneliness chimed in, "Stay and enjoy the conversation."

An hour went by. Conscience pulled at me. "You're still here? I thought you had reading to do."

There's nothing wrong with spending time with a friend, and he's not busy today; he said so.

Loneliness piped in. "You'll have to bury him, you know. You'll have to bury all the people you've met here. You're moving in June, remember? They all must go. Chris, Dency, Monie, Andy, Joyce, Harris, Jackie, and Ron. You're already grieving and digging their graves. That's one of the storms raging inside you."

I stood my ground. *No! I've put down roots eleven times, only to have them ripped out of the soil. It isn't fair! I'm not doing that again. I won't.*

Ron once again took my hand in his before I left. When I was out of sight, I held that hand before my face, examining my fingers.

I have dry roots. I'm thirsty for a genuine connection with others. "Loneliness?"

"Yes?"

"*Burying relationships that could have developed into deep friendships really hurts.*"

"I know."

Several days later, I stopped by Ron's office but was extremely uncomfortable with the neon sign flashing on and off over my head advertising *Pathetic, Lonely, Woman.* I left shortly after I arrived, saying to myself, "I'm not going to see him again."

But the following week, my feet took me there anyway—*damn traitors.* My throat hurt, and my head ached. I shouldn't have been there infecting his office with my germs, but he took my mind off the pain with his humor and conversation.

Driving home after my evening class, Conscience had a few things to say. "You're leading him on. You're not an innocent girl in junior high. You know what your frequent visits imply."

*You're wrong! I don't feel that way. He's just a guy from class.
He knows I'm married.*

Logic forced its way into the conversation. "It doesn't
change a thing."

Conscience saw its opportunity to hurl another insult.
"You're a tease. You don't even know you're doing it because
you're too damn friendly."

Loneliness came to my defense. "If her husband wasn't
preoccupied with this move and finding another job, maybe he
would pay more attention to her. It's his fault."

"Don't blame other people for your unhappiness," Logic
added. "That was the first thing you learned when you decided
to become an independent woman instead of a codependent
wife. You're responsible for your happiness; don't forget that!"

I wiped my tears and blew my nose after parking the car. It
was nearing eleven o'clock. Good thing the lights were off in
the house. I didn't want Donn to see my swollen red eyes from
fifty miles of tears. Worse, my throat was on fire, and my head
felt hot. I probably had strep throat again.

I crawled into bed but couldn't rest. When I finally dozed
off, it was a fitful sleep. I walked past old graves, remembering,
grieving, and reading the headstones of people I'd connected
with but had to leave behind because we moved away: Dee,
Jenny, Carleen, Faith, Karma, and Pat.

I awoke, holding back sobs as more grief engulfed me.
Grabbing the tissue box on my nightstand, I went into the living room, sat on the sofa, and stared at my withered thirsty
hand.

"What is it that you want?" Loneliness asked.

I want to feel loved. I want to be held. I want close friends.

"But you are responsible for your happiness," Logic scolded.

"You don't need anyone else."

I hurled the tissue box across the room. *Shut up and leave me alone!*

Then I curled up on the sofa, mourning those I'd buried and those who would be next.

CHAPTER 22

Endings Create Beginnings

HUMANS INSTINCTIVELY KNOW WHEN SOMETHING NEEDS to change in their lives. Our bodies alert us with neck and shoulder pain, headaches, clenched teeth, stress, fatigue, and other health issues. Our emotions tell us with frustration, doubt, worry, anger, insecurity, guilt, fear, despair, and powerlessness.

We might not know how to remedy the situation, but we definitely know when something doesn't feel right. Sometimes we know exactly what to do, but we come up with a multitude of excuses to ignore our instincts.

My intuition shouted, "Leave the marriage," but I never said aloud that I wanted a divorce, even though it had been simmering on low for our entire marriage. It was apparent that neither of us was happy, and our few marriage counseling sessions came too late.

I didn't want to be the one to end our marriage. I kept hoping Donn would bring it up first, and then one day, he did. I was thrilled beyond belief. Unfortunately, a week later, he changed his mind.

Dammit!

So I did research on ending a marriage. Dr. Dan Kiley's book *Living Together, Feeling Alone* addressed the myth that we must physically be alone to feel alone. What jumped out at me

163

was that loneliness is caused by a lack of self-love. And when we don't have self-love, we hand our power over to others.

As a child, my parents were the authority in my life. At the naïve age of eighteen, I foolishly married someone I barely knew and turned my blossoming independent female power over to someone else because Christianity said the man was the head of the house.

Dr. Kiley spoke directly to my heart, and when I returned to college, I slowly began finding my power in the world. However, in my home life, I was so concerned about how a divorce would affect my family that I was willing to sacrifice my happiness for theirs. It was killing me emotionally.

Then I read *Coming Apart: Why Relationships End and How to Live Through the Ending of Yours* by Daphne Rose Kingma.

I learned from Kingma's book that no matter how happy or dysfunctional one's childhood is, we are never fully prepared to be on our own. So, we form relationships: friends, roommates, coworkers, lovers, marriage partners, etc., and in those interactions, we figure out who we are and what we want. However, those relationships are not meant to be for life.

I did research into the phrase *til death do us part*. It first appeared in the Christian Book of Common Prayer in 1549. Back then, if you weren't one of the 25 percent who died before age five or one of the 40 percent who died before age fifteen, your life expectancy was only thirty-five. A spouse dying from an accident, infection, disease, or childbirth was common. Families stayed together for survival, not because the writers of the Book of Common Prayer (not God) decreed that marriage was for life.

Fortunately, we don't live in the 1500s. We can learn and grow from our interactions with others and have the option to move on when our paths go in different directions. When matrimony ends, it doesn't always mean the relationship failed. It can also mean that it succeeded.

I was now a leader instead of a follower and had my own opinions. I was a published writer, a mother of three wonderful children, and in a month, I would finally have a college degree, precisely twenty years after graduating from high school. This was a significant accomplishment. From this perspective, our marriage was a success. I knew in my heart that it was time for me to move on, and with this knowledge, I found the voice to say aloud, "I want a divorce."

Thirty years later, as I wrote this book, Donn and I would spend time emailing and talking on the phone about our years in the ministry, which added several scenes and more details to this memoir. In one of his emails, he wrote, "I was such an unsettled idiot, always interrupting family to do other things. You had so much to give, yet I never took the time to appreciate or support you the way you deserved. You were amazing, though I probably never told you."

In May of 1991, I was in the twentieth graduating class at SSU with a 3.74 grade point average for the three semesters.

Whoop-whoop! Way to go, Gaye!

My parents, sisters, Donn, and our children were there to see me walk across the stage and applaud my accomplishment. (Four years later, SSU was acquired by the University of Illinois and became a four-year college now known as the University of Illinois Springfield.)

Even though divorce was forthcoming, Donn and I had a family to support. We wanted all five of us to survive, so we stayed together as those families did in the 1500s. We moved to Springfield, where an older couple we knew offered us their finished basement for as long as we needed until we found jobs and a place to live.

With my office background, getting steady temp jobs through an employment agency was easy, especially when I typed over eighty words a minute. Donn worked at a Farm and Home store for three months. In August, we had an apartment, and Donn had a full-time job teaching music at a public elementary school.

We went our separate ways in November, as separate as a couple can be living in the same small town and sharing children.

When United Methodist clergy are going through a divorce, they must consult with the bishop and their district superintendent. As Donn's spouse, I received a letter inviting me to this meeting.

I remember a few things I wrote when I replied to the invite. "I am not clergy. I was never an employee of a church. I did not receive support from the conference. I don't owe them an explanation for why I am getting divorced. I'm not attending this meeting."

Donn told me that at the end of the session, the representatives asked him, "What can we do for you?"

He had the good sense to say, "You're too late."

The conference now requires ministers to have a mentor, someone to work with and hold them accountable, rather than being left alone to figure out how to balance family and church. Getting tossed into the pool's deep end without a life jacket isn't the best way to learn how to swim.

We divorced on June 16, 1992, one day before what would have been our twentieth anniversary.

* * *

I was now making decent money working full-time for an insurance broker. When the children were with their dad every other weekend, I had time to get to know Ron better. He was gentle and kind with a great sense of humor, a dimpled smile, and that deep warm maple syrup bedroom voice.

We hadn't been together long when he confessed, "I was drawn to you that first day of class the moment I heard your voice as you stood to read your story. Then I heard you laugh. You sounded like an angel. I leaned back in my chair to see you better. My eyes went from your face down your body to your hand resting on the table to the wedding ring on your finger, and I thought—dammit! When Jackie handed you the blindfold and told you to pick a partner, I sat there saying to myself, pick me, pick me—and you did!"

At first, Ron was more serious about me than I was about him. I wasn't used to having so much male attention. When we attended the Army-Navy band performance at the Sangamon Auditorium, everyone watched the musicians except Ron, who sat googly-eyed, gazing at me.

I quietly reprimanded him three times during the concert, "Stop staring at me!"

He held my hand in public. He listened intently to my every word and always opened doors for me. He kept an extra sweatshirt and jacket in his car in case I got cold. His six-foot-tall slim build and my five-foot-four height enabled my head to fit perfectly in the hollow of his shoulder. His plaid cotton shirts absorbed at least a million tears as I went through the divorce and the year following. My initial embarrassment with his attention quickly faded. This man's love, respect, and support earned him the right to gaze at me as much as he wanted.

Ron and I had been dating for about three years when I bought my first house, a cute three-bedroom ranch with a two-car garage. The one thing I didn't like was the ugly overgrown shrubbery blocking the walkway in front of the house.

"I really hate these bushes," I complained.

Having heard my parsonage nightmare stories, he commented, "You don't need permission to get rid of them. You own the house."

"Oh my gosh! You're right!"

Giddy with the sense of house freedom, my mind went wild. "I can tear down walls, add another room, paint the house purple—or orange—and no one can stop me!"

"I'll pull the bushes out for you," Ron offered.

"You're the best!"

This man was amazing. I loved him, but I had jumped from living with my parents into a relationship with Donn, followed almost immediately by a relationship with Ron.

I was forty-one years old and still had no idea what it was like to live alone. My children were at Donn's every other weekend. I wanted that time to experience life on my own terms without considering anyone else's needs. I didn't think that was too much to ask.

Devastated, Ron asked, "How much time do you need?"

I didn't know what to say. All I knew was that I desperately needed some space. Ron honored my request for the most part, but not entirely.

I wasn't surprised when he showed up at the house with a shovel in hand a few weeks later to pull out the shrubbery. To be honest, I was relieved to see him. What single woman in her right mind would turn down free manual labor?

Then on a sweltering July evening, he invited me out on

his fishing boat, knowing full well that my kids would be at their dad's and that bobbing on the water while stargazing and listening to the distant sounds of laughter and crackling camp-fires was one of my favorite things to do. Sneaky! I said yes but kept my distance in the boat.

He stopped by again in late August to say hello, and before he left, he hugged me. His deep sexy voice, as he whispered, "I miss you," mingled with the smell of his Black Suede cologne, reminded me of how safe I always felt when in his arms.

What the heck! I was never gonna have space until my kids left home anyway. Why not hang out with a man who loves me and smells good? Ron still refers to this separation as the sum-mer from hell.

Being with Ron was exciting. He worked part-time at an oldies (1960s and 1970s) radio station. When he got off work at midnight, I'd meet him and his friends at Chantilly Lace, a dance bar. Going out in the middle of the night was thrilling. Ron gave me all the experiences I had missed when I married a minister at eighteen.

By our sixth year of dating, I was juggling three teenagers at home and a full-time clerical job. By the end of the week, I was typically exhausted and that was when Ron would call to discuss plans for the weekend.

"What would you like to do tonight?" Ron's cheerful voice echoed through my work phone.

"I don't know."

"Do you want me to meet you at your house, and we'll decide later?"

"I don't know!" I snapped, which was unusual.

An inspired thought then popped into my head. "Let's get married," I said as if I'd casually suggested we go to a movie.

Silence on the other end of the phone. Then, "Are you sure?"

"Yes, I'm sure. I want us to go to the same house at the end of the day without discussing it first. And then I want to stay home and do nothing—together. Dating is too much work."

"But what about your space?"

"Space is overrated, plus I need dental work, and you have better insurance."

"So, you want me for my health benefits." Pause. "I can go along with that."

We married four months later, on May 31, 1997. Within three weeks, I had two new dental fillings and a crown replaced.

Spiritualist/ Baptist/Israel

AFTER OUR WEDDING ON THE BACK deck of my house, we drove to Cornucopia in northern Wisconsin to the one-room cottage my grandparents built on Lake Superior in the 1950s. It was now owned by my aunt, who graciously let us use it for our honeymoon. I spent many weeks there with my family when I was growing up.

Cornucopia is an unincorporated community with about ninety-eight people, three churches, a general store, a restaurant, and several bars; it was named for the mythical "horn of plenty" for its abundant natural resources. Ron and I were going to lay low, hang out around the house, read on the beach, take walks, wade in the frigid lake, and enjoy each other's company.

As we drove north to our destination, Ron said, "I brought a box of books I thought might interest you. They're on the back seat if you want to take a look."

Cool! A cornucopia of new ideas!

I was immediately drawn to a book about the zodiac and amazed at how accurately my sign described me.

"A person under the sign of Cancer (me) is learning through feelings and emotions. They are natural nurturers, loyal and protective of those they love. They are sensitive to what others feel and can unknowingly absorb those feelings into themselves. Because of this sensitivity, they need the security of a harmonious home where they feel safe to go within themselves, not to hide but to find inner balance through the power of mind, soul, and spirit."

You're probably wondering how I jumped from the Bible to the zodiac. That happened during the six years between the two marriages.

~ THE SIX YEARS ~

Before I met Ron, I had already begun to question religion, and after the Holy Spirit/Force experience, I saw myself as spiritual, not religious. Even so, I still wanted a Sunday morning church service, so I started church hopping, and Ron tagged along.

Ron grew up in the Christian church, served as a junior deacon, and still attended church on occasion when he wasn't working one of his three jobs: the university, the radio station, or at the Navy Reserve Center, where Chief Petty Officer Kick served as a classroom instructor.

I was still serving on the Conference Deaf and Hearing-Impaired Ministry Board when a Springfield Methodist church started a Sunday morning service for the deaf in their chapel. Because of my musical background and four years studying American Sign Language, I was asked to interpret the music. I thoroughly enjoyed my part in this ministry, but my time on the board was ending. I longed to try other churches and hopefully hear a sermon I hadn't heard a thousand times.

I had one more commitment to fulfill before my term ended: to speak at a United Methodist Church seventy-five miles northeast about the Deaf and Hearing-Impaired ministry.

Ron came along as my chauffeur.

After my gig at the church, he drove us around the town of thirty-five hundred people, where we discovered a spiritualist church.

"Let's go in!" Ron suggested.

"Oh, I don't know," I said, pulling the Bible I used during the church service into my arms.

"It will be fine," he encouraged.

"Okay, but let's pray first." I took his hand and prayed out loud for protection. I even carried the Bible into the building with me.

There was nothing unusual about the service. The songs were the same ones I'd been singing for years. The huge difference came at the end of the service when the minister, an older adult, gave a few of the attendees a personal message from deceased loved ones.

He came to me first. "May I speak with you?"

"Sure!" I said with a gulp.

"I have a grandmother coming to you. Do you have a grandmother who has passed?"

"Yes."

"I'm getting the name Mary. Was that her name?"

"No."

"She keeps saying that name. You may understand why later. She says you are thinking about changing jobs or adding another job."

Stunned, I replied, "Yes."

"Your grandmother says to do it. It will be very good for you."

WOW!!! This was amazing. It certainly qualified as hearing something new from the pulpit. And to think I almost missed it because I was scared of a different kind of church.

After the service, we went downstairs for refreshments, and the minister showed us the séance room. It was a small room, about twelve feet by ten feet, with no windows and a small desk in the corner with an old, beige push-button telephone.

Curious, Ron asked, "So, what's up with the telephone? Do the spirits call the message in?"

The minister chuckled. "No, it's just a phone on my desk."

I connected the name Mary the following day when I decided to go ahead and sign up to be a Mary Kay beauty consultant. Grandma was right. It was good for me.

What I remember most about my three years with Mary Kay was the camaraderie and the encouragement to use visualization to manifest our goals. My goal was to quit my job, sell Mary Kay products full-time, and drive a pink Cadillac. I never got the car or the full-time job, but visualization did become a part of my everyday life, not just my prayer life.

When our friend Tim told us about a newly formed Baptist church that met in the basement of an office building, my kids, Ron, and I attended. We enjoyed connecting with the thirty attendees, the young minister, his wife, and their children. I even liked his sermons, but three months in, he said that according to the Bible, dinosaurs roamed the earth six thousand years ago.

What? Maybe he had never heard of carbon dating, which has scientifically proven that dinosaurs lived millions of years ago.

When I asked the minister if I could sing a solo for the church service, he said, "You can sing, but only men can speak from the pulpit."

Excuse me? Did we jump back to the Dark Ages?

"I'm also interested in teaching Sunday school. I've taught every age from nursery to adult."

"We'd love to have you, but women can only teach the children. And you'd have to join the church. Have you been baptized by immersion?" he questioned. "It's a requirement."

All these rules were starting to piss me off. "I was sprinkled as a baby, but I will be baptized by immersion in the Jordon River next month—the one in Israel." That little addition at the end was me trying to be snarky.

"If you're not baptized by a minister associated with our Baptist denomination, you won't be accepted."

The Jordan River, where Jesus was baptized, isn't good enough? I bet this Baptist headquarters is the same one that determined I had too many issues to be a missionary.

Going to Israel wasn't my idea. My parents had scheduled a Holy Land tour with a televangelist faith healer they were following after my thirteen-year-old nephew was seriously injured in a car accident. His brain injury left him bedridden, unable to move or talk, and needing a feeding tube.

Eight months before the Israel trip, my dad died. He had just come home from building another cabin in the mountains of Gatlinburg when he suddenly doubled over with a horrible stomachache.

Trying to find a cause for his distress, Mom asked, "What did you eat when you got home from work?"

"The usual," he answered. "A hot dog and a martini."

Mom called 911 when he passed out for a few seconds. When the ambulance arrived and took his blood pressure, Dad asked, "What are my BP numbers?"

The EMT replied, "Forty."

"Forty over what?" Dad questioned.

"Forty over nothing."

"No shit?" he replied.

"We're calling Life Star to helicopter you to Knoxville."

"No shit?" Dad said again. Those were his last words.

He had an abdominal aortic aneurysm. No matter how many times the doctor repaired the aorta during surgery, it burst open in another spot. Dad was moved to the ICU, where my mother and friends from their Walk to Emmaus spiritual community gathered around his bed, singing praise songs as he made his transition to the other side on March 24, 1994, at age sixty-five.

It rained for two days after his death, and it was still storming the evening of the memorial service. As we headed to and from the service, the rivers flowing through Gatlinburg were dangerously close to cresting. We had just returned to the condo when we heard on the news that the roads were now closed. And then the electricity went out, plunging us into darkness.

The sons-in-law and Ron stumbled to the fireplace and were surprised that Dad had already prepared the logs for the next time they were needed. All they had to do was strike the match.

Mom pulled me aside a few days later. "Your dad and I already paid to go to Israel in November."

"Oh, that's right! Are you still going to go? I think you should," I urged.

She smiled. "I am, and you're coming with me."

A week later, Mom called to thank the people who stood with her when Dad died. When she thanked the couple at the foot of the bed, they replied, "We weren't there. We were out of town."

So who was at the foot of Dad's bed? Angels? Deceased relatives in disguise who knew Mom would eventually discover their presence when she said her thank-yous? I can't answer that question, but I know someone from the other side was there.

Now that Mom and I had both been on a Walk to Emmaus retreat, we were on the same Holy Spirit jargon wavelength and had fun touring Israel with a group of two hundred, divided into ten tour buses with twenty people per bus. I was forty-one, and Mom was sixty-four.

While in Jerusalem, we visited the Western Wall, also known as the Wailing Wall. The site has two sections for prayer, one for women and one for men, with a short dividing wall between the two. When one of the seventy men gathered for prayer came over to where we stood outside the men's section to say hello, a woman from our tour bus started witnessing for Jesus.

Oy vey!

I was embarrassed to be standing beside her. We were at the most religious site in the world for the Jewish population, yet she had the gall to tell the man he wasn't going to heaven unless he gave his life to Jesus. The man smiled at her disrespectful comment and kindly added, "I disagree," before nodding and walking away.

Part of our Holy Land tour included spiritual services. Whenever the faith healer prayed, random people around us would fall, either to their chairs or the floor. In a large outdoor venue overlooking the Old City and the Judean Hills, the people in all twelve rows in front of Mom and me fell into their chairs one row at a time, like dominos, leaving the last two rows standing, which was good because the woman in front of me almost missed her chair, and I was there to catch her.

She and many others appeared to be drunk afterward.

Concerned that the woman might fall off the chair, I put my hands on her shoulders for about five minutes until she came out of the trance. After the service, she thanked me and added, "I felt energy throughout my body coming from your hands. It was amazing. Thank you."

She felt that from me?

In Nazareth, our tour bus had the opportunity to have a prayer service in a small church made entirely of stone, inside and out. The room we were in was no bigger than fifteen feet by fifteen feet, with a stone ledge for sitting placed around three of the walls and a white marble altar on the fourth wall.

"Does anyone want prayer while we're here?" asked our bus leader. "If so, come to the middle of the room, and we'll lay hands on you."

I was surprised that Mom went forward, but then I realized she was there for my nephew, her grandson, who needed healing. The other eighteen people immediately swarmed around her, each person happily buzzing their prayers out loud, like a colony of bees on a honeycomb.

I was too far back to lay my hands on her, so I sat on the stone ledge. Five minutes later, the group was still praying.

Why are they taking so long?

My intuition said they wouldn't stop until she fell over, which she finally did. When they picked her up off the floor, she wore a goofy smirk. Pulling me aside as the others left the building, she whispered, "I finally fell down to make them happy. I figured we'd be there all day if I didn't."

My mother is a hoot.

On the morning of the last day, we had a calm boat ride on the Sea of Galilee—the lowest freshwater lake on Earth. The sun was shining, and the water was smooth and blue. It was much smaller than I expected, only eight miles wide and twelve miles long, surrounded by a rocky shore and hills. It was the most peaceful boat ride that I've ever experienced.

That afternoon, following the water excursion, we headed to Yardenit on the Jordan River, one of the possible baptismal sites of Jesus. Crossing over the river on our way reminded me of the Sangamon River, a tributary of the Illinois River that flows north of Springfield with lush green trees and shrubbery on each shore. I expected it to be bigger.

The baptismal site had a gift shop and concrete bleachers for spectators. We were given a white robe and towel, then led to the locker rooms, where we changed into our bathing suits and covered them with our robes. Our group then headed to the river, walking on a smooth rock path into and out of the water. The trail within the water had a fence separating the baptism site from the rest of the river.

Can't have recently baptized Christians floating away now, can we?

It took a long time for the evangelist to baptize two hundred people. I thought we would never get our turn. When we finally reached the evangelist, Mom walked toward him, but before turning around so he could lean her back into the water, she fell into the water face first, as if she was in a trance, just like all those people at the healing services. I thought she had a spiritual experience, but when she came back up, she acted as if nothing had happened. According to Mom, she wanted a spiritual experience, but to this day, she believes the evangelist lost his grip, and she slid out of his hands.

My experience was anticlimactic compared to hers. I was dunked, came out of the water, and walked away. *Ho-hum.* I could have stayed home and been immersed in the small

Baptist church's horse tank they brought into the building for baptisms. This was the Jordan River, for crying out loud! I expected more.

I'd seen enough ruins and religious sites to last a lifetime, and there were still more on the schedule before arriving at the airport for our midnight flight to New York. Exhausted and disappointed, I desperately needed to cry but couldn't because Mom was obsessing about what she would do with her wet hair when her curling iron was inside her luggage under the bus.

I've said before that when you want something and think you can't have it, the solution is probably right in front of you or very close at hand. There was a woman on the bus using a battery-operated curling iron. She happily loaned it to Mom along with a small mirror, which I held as Mom fussed with her hair.

Five weeks after we returned from Israel, the Baptist minister packed up his family and moved away without giving notice. The church was officially closed the Sunday before Christmas.

I swear, I had nothing to do with him leaving! At least, I don't think so.

Assembly of God/ Holy Spirit Movement

THE NEXT SPRINGFIELD CHURCH WAS ASSEMBLY of God, which also met in a space owned by a business. They spoke openly about the Holy Spirit, and when they prayed for someone, they laid hands on them, like the prayer team at the Walk to Emmaus retreat but not as zealous as our bus mates in Israel.

I joined a small group that met at a church member's home once a week. Several group members believed that the Holy Spirit lived within us, not outside of us. That was new to me, but it made sense. Why would we think we are separate from God when Jesus said the Kingdom of God was within us?

One night at the group, I asked for prayer. I was dealing with a coworker and needed the courage to stand up to them. The group laid hands on me and began to pray. At one point, I wondered why everyone was praying so loud until I realized I was making all the noise.

Did I pick that up in Israel?

My arms and legs began to tingle, so much so that I had difficulty standing. And then, I found myself on the floor, lying on my back.

Why didn't this happen at the Jordan River?

A woman who always carried an oversized King James Bible started talking about me as if I had just died or was in a coma.

"What just happened to Gaye? Was she slain in the Spirit?" she asked.

I felt tranquil lying on the floor, listening to the many questions and answers, and then an overwhelming unconditional love for everyone in the room poured over me. If I could've gotten off the floor, I would've pulled them one by one into my arms and whispered, "It's all good. Let it go."

I wasn't the least bit concerned about what anyone thought of me. It was as if I had reached a higher plane where the actions and thoughts of others had no effect on me. That's when I began to laugh. Not little tee-hee laughter or chuckles, but big, unstoppable belly laughs that spilled out of me so intensely that my stomach muscles were sore the next day.

If this was the Holy Spirit laughing through me, it was having a ball. Maybe it had been sipping communion wine all afternoon.

The following Sunday, during worship, the minister said, "Some of you may have heard about what happened this past week in one of the small groups. I want to assure you that this will not happen during worship."

I visualized the Holy Spirit handcuffed and dragged from the altar down the aisle and out the front door. As he passed me, he shrugged his shoulders as if to say, *Oh, Well. Maybe next time.*

I left this church the following week, and like the little Baptist church before it, this one also closed its doors.

Again, not my fault.

There was a huge outpouring of the Holy Spirit between 1995 and 1999, with several churches in the area experiencing this phenomenon. I attended all of them at one time or another but found one in particular I liked the best.

An hour before the service, they played CDs by musicians who were a part of the Holy Spirit movement. The lyrics and melodies were alive with positive spiritual energy. My hands tingled as my soul danced.

Freedom during worship was refreshing. We were encouraged to do whatever the Holy Spirit led us to do during the church services: sit, stand, sway, raise our arms, lay on the floor, or run through the sanctuary. It took me a while before I was comfortable standing and raising my hands above my head, but I never ran around the room or lay on the floor.

One Sunday, the minister said, "If the Holy Spirit tells you to leave the sanctuary and call or visit someone, don't hesitate. Get up from your seat and do what you are being led to do."

Freedom to follow my spiritual guidance—during a church service? Epic!

The minister encouraged developing one's intuition. We stood in a circle at a weekend workshop with one person standing in the middle. We were to focus on them and listen to what our intuition was telling us. Then we each had the opportunity to tell the person what we intuitively saw for them. In turn, they told us if it meant something to them. I was surprised by my accuracy.

For that same event, the church brought in what they called prophets, who were said to speak on behalf of God. I went forward to the front of the church along with others to have their hands laid on me. One of the prophets placed his hands on my head, then quickly stepped back to look at me, announcing, "The Lord really likes you!"

How does one reply to something like that?

The only response I could think of was, "I like Him too."

I never doubted that God liked me, but it was nice to have

confirmation, like a note passed in elementary school: "Do you like me? Yes or No."

"He's very jealous over you. He's giving you dreams and visions. Have you been dreaming?"

"Oh yeah!"

I worked part-time as the director of a children's supper program at a United Methodist Church. Our volunteer cook was a formidable woman in her forties who was very protective of the children in her neighborhood. Her voice was harsh when she spoke to them about being alert when playing outside. We got along fine, but she scared me a little bit.

In my dream, she had scissors for fingers, and when she pushed the children behind her to protect them from two bad guys, she inadvertently injured them. This dream helped me to see her as someone who genuinely cared about the children in the neighborhood. She used the only tool in her bag, her loud, sharp, severe voice, to keep them safe and scare them into listening to her wisdom.

When I went with friends to another Holy Spirit church where a guest prophet spoke, I was smart enough to bring my cassette tape recorder. (This was before cell phones had voice recorders.)

He said, "The Lord says you ask why a lot."

Uh oh! My oldest child used to ask "why" all the time. It drove me nuts.

"God says: I will give you answers for yourself and others. For yourself, it will be okay, but for others, you will wonder if you should tell them what you know. The Lord will teach you to discern when to hold back, when to just pray, and when to speak the word. The Lord is giving you an understanding of His written and spoken Word. You're going to say, 'This is relevant to this over here, and this goes with that.' God says you should be ready to receive more of my Word, not less."

During my Holy Spirit exploration, I watched many people falling into the aisles and lying on the floor through an entire service. The rest of us just stepped around and over them. I was knocked down two more times in two different churches. It hasn't happened since, which is good because it's not as easy for me to get off the floor as it once was.

Ron and I got married in my—now our—backyard. The ceremony was informal. Ron wore his signature blue jeans and a button-down-the-front, short-sleeved cotton blue-and-white-striped shirt. I bought a cute blue-and-white-flowered cotton sundress on sale at Kmart. After the ceremony, I sold over a hundred dollars of Mary Kay products while the burgers were cooking on the grill.

Even though Ron was a seeker of knowledge, he didn't care much for the Holy Spirit church, and they didn't like him either. He asked too many questions, such as, "How did the soul get stuffed into these bodies?" And he made comments like, "The Bible isn't all it's cracked up to be."

In September, the minister called us into his office and asked Ron, "What does being a Christian mean to you?"

Ron answered, "It means following the teachings of Jesus Christ." According to the minister, that was the wrong answer, and he asked Ron to leave the church.

I was stunned and angry, not just because my new husband was kicked out but because I was invited to stay! I knew what happens when one person puts a church before their spouse, and I had the divorce papers to prove it.

At this point, I'd given mainstream religion forty-four years of my life. I'd worshipped and sang in many churches, meeting many wonderful people, but I'd had enough of the constraints of religion and each individual minister's interpretation of it. I wanted freedom from religion, but I also wanted to have a spiritual life.

The six years Ron and I dated opened my eyes to many new and unusual experiences. By the time we headed north to Cornucopia for our honeymoon, I was thrilled to read the zodiac book.

As we settled into married life, on Sunday nights at eleven o'clock, Ron listened to Art Bell's radio show *Coast to Coast*, where people called in to talk about weird things like UFOs and Area 51. I wasn't interested in aliens, but I listened along with Ron if a guest was talking about anything paranormal.

I heard Dannion Brinkley, author of *Saved by the Light: The True Story of a Man Who Died Twice and the Profound Revelations He Received*, talk about his three near-death experiences: one from lightning and two more during surgeries. Another time, I listened in fascination as Dr. Bruce Goldberg, an international hypnotherapist and author, spoke about how we can have out-of-body experiences. I even wrote down something he said: "Fear is the F word of spiritual growth."

I know from personal experience that most religions tell people what they should and shouldn't do, but how do we know if we agree with a topic if we don't investigate it ourselves?

I had no fear as I explored these new ideas that presented themselves. I read books on mind, body, spirit, higher consciousness, psychics, crystals, astrology, numerology, quantum physics, the soul, spiritual gifts, channeling, chakras, Reiki healing, intuition, and the Law of Attraction, to name a few. Ron and I even took a tarot class together at the local community college.

Like the instructor I had for the Credit for Prior Learning class at SSU, I started using tarot cards at home. If I was chewing on an issue or felt out of sorts, I'd shuffle the deck, pull a random card, and then use a tarot handbook to understand what the card meant. I'd take that information and journal about how it applied to what was happening in my life. After several pages of writing, I could see my situation from a new angle, allowing me to change my perspective. I still use the cards, but not very often anymore.

Like Shirley MacLaine in her mid-forties, I also was having a thrilling spiritual journey reading every metaphysical book I could get my hands on and awakening to a higher consciousness of who I am in the universe.

CHAPTER 25

Spiritualism

FIVE MONTHS AFTER OUR WEDDING IN 1997, Ron said, "Why don't we check out that spiritualist church again?"

Road trip!

According to the National Spiritualist Association of Churches, "Spiritualism is a scientific, philosophical religion that embraces the science of life, the philosophy of existence, and the religion of humanity, based upon communication through mediumship with those in the Spirit World."

They have no dogma or creeds and believe people are responsible for their happiness or unhappiness as they obey or disobey natural and spiritual laws. God is referred to as Infinite Intelligence. I liked that name.

On the Sunday we attended, we were told that the minister who had laughed with Ron in the séance room several years earlier had passed away. Various guest mediums were filling the pulpit until a new minister was found.

After the service, as I scanned a bookcase in the basement just outside the séance room, I pulled out a small five-by-seven-inch blue book titled *Becoming a Spiritualist* by H. Gordon Burroughs and randomly opened the book to page fifteen. These words caught my attention:

"It [Spiritualism] enables the seeker after truth, to realize that man is a soul now, animated by spirit, a dweller in ever-present eternity, and that he is co-eternal with God, occupying a physical body through which he manifests on the earth plane. Man is not a body with a spirit, but a spirit with a body and a mind to serve him. Man is not going to eternity after the change called death; he is living in eternity now" (Burroughs 1962, 15).

Oh, my gosh! This made so much sense.

My body doesn't have a Soul. I am the Soul. Mind-blowing!

When we returned three months later, I met an art teacher who said she was painting spirit pictures. She meditates on a person's name, then, with Spirit's guidance, she paints a picture, not of the person's face they see in the mirror but of their soul's essence and journey. I'm not an impulse buyer, but I opened my purse and pulled out my checkbook. "How much for a painting?"

"I haven't been doing it very long, so it's only twenty dollars," she explained.

Sweet! I expected to pay more.

I handed her the check, telling her nothing about myself except my first and middle names. Weeks later, when the painting was finished, she gave it to me at church.

The painting was enchanting, with a deep orange and red background. In the center was the pale face of a young woman with a circle in the middle of her forehead, just above the eyebrows. She wore a headdress with rays of color: deep red, purple, and lavender, laden with what looked like golden coins. On her chest was a gold heart radiating white and pink light. Below the heart were a quill pen and a blue open book with my name above in bold black calligraphy lettering.

Then the artist handed me a piece of paper with a handwritten channeled message she had received after finishing the painting.

My child, my child, you are blessed. Have you forgotten this? You have work to do, and it is to begin. DO NOT TARRY any longer. Tune in to the energy through your spiritual painting. It is a conduit, so place it in a space of reverence and action (for writing). This is your mission, your assignment...You are to bless hearts, many hearts, by spreading God's word by being yourself but also as a channel for Spirit.

DO NOT TARRY, my child. The time is now. Take up the quill as pictured and spread the message of truth, hope, and love to all light beings. This is your gift to life...So be it. Go in peace, harmony, and love, my dearest child of God. The angels rejoice with you in your next venture (adventure)!

I was shocked when I saw the book and quill. The artist didn't know I was once a published writer with visions of writing again. I put the spirit painting in a frame and hung it on the wall of my pink and purple home office, which once served as my Mary Kay office before I realized selling cosmetics was not my passion. Occasionally, I would look at the painting and read the message, thinking, "I wonder what I will write someday that will bless many hearts?"

Ron and I found the church very interesting, but getting there and back took three hours, plus an additional two hours for the service and discussion afterward, so we only attended a few times.

A few years passed when Ron again suggested, "Let's go to the spiritualist church this Sunday."

The congregation had grown with a new minister and his wife, who was also a medium and attending school to become a spiritualist minister. With the two of them, the church was alive with good vibes. We began attending once a month.

I took a correspondence course on the History of Spiritualism and served as a guest speaker once for Sunday service. I considered becoming a spiritualist minister until I remembered my experience with the well-intentioned dragons. Plus, I would have to become a medium. I wasn't ready for that.

We had weird things happening at home when Ron and I attended this church. We would smell cotton candy and popcorn at random times of the day. When I noticed these smells, I would say aloud, "Hello? Hello? If you're trying to tell me something, I apologize that I don't understand, but you're welcome to hang around as long as you like."

One morning, we awoke to find Ron's work boots on the kitchen floor, one shoe standing up and the other lying beside it with white powder sprinkled on both. When we entered the garage, his other work boots were in the same position with the same powder sprinkles.

We got to experience the séance room, which was as dark as when I toured the Mammoth Cave, and the lights were turned off for a minute to demonstrate just how *dark* dark is.

In the séance room, Ron and I sat blind, waiting for something to happen. Once, there was a quick flash of light in the middle of the room, which was pretty exciting. Of course, someone in the room could have flicked a lighter, but I doubt it. The rest of the attendees were hardcore spiritualists.

When the minister demonstrated table-turning (also known as table-tipping, table-tapping, and table-tilting) with a lightweight table the size of a TV tray, I was not impressed. However, I saw a table in action when I attended a spiritualist women's retreat.

The retreat center had a huge heavy oak pedestal table, large enough to seat twelve people. I know it was weighty because I was one of eight women who struggled to move it to the middle of the room. The other attendees took turns standing around the table with only their fingertips on the surface. I watched in amazement from the sidelines as that table stumbled like a drunken soldier eight feet from where it started.

As I watched the table dance, I sensed my dad sitting next to me, so I asked, "Why aren't you moving the table?"

"I have more important things to do than move furniture," he replied. Yep, that was definitely my father. We sat together until I felt him leave, and then I went to bed.

One of my favorite things about the spiritualist church was the confirmation that I wasn't imagining the strong connection I felt with my dad. He came to me through the church's spirit greetings, and so have my grandparents, father-in-law, uncle, nephew, and one of my singing coaches, who stopped by two months after she passed away.

Whether I do or don't receive a message during a church service, I'm always touched by the spirit greetings of others, especially when the medium gives undeniable evidence that the spirit coming through is a loved one. I've seen hundreds of these greetings that have been emotionally healing to the receiver, especially when a parent, unable to express love in the physical world, apologizes and asks for forgiveness.

We weren't official church members, but we happened by chance (*or was it?*) to attend one Sunday when it was time for the annual meeting. Everyone was signing their membership card for the year, so we signed a card, too. It was also time to vote for the new board members.

"We have one open spot that needs to be filled on the board, that of treasurer," said the president. "Does anyone have a nomination?"

The minister's wife chimed in, "I nominate Gaye."

"Gaye, do you accept the nomination?" The president asked.

I love accounting with its checks and balances. Before I had a chance to fully consider the ramifications of once again knowing every tiny detail of a church, the good and the bad, my ego piped up with a gushing, "I'd love to!"

When we got in the car to drive home, I said, "How am I going to tell my mom that I'm a card-carrying spiritualist and a board member?"

"Don't tell her. It's not like she knows we've been coming here."

True!

When I asked Ron what he felt about being a spiritualist, he said, "When I was growing up, I went to many churches, my own and my friends'. Each church was okay, but there was no sense of exploration. They told me what to believe: This is it, and there's no more.

"You can't go any further when you've been told there is a barrier; heaven and hell are over there, and you're over here. If you're a good person, you go to heaven. If you're a bad person, you go to hell. It's a finite set of rules. There's a line drawn, and we're told there's no way to cross it to explore anything else because the line says there is nothing else.

"With the spiritualist church and other places like that, there is an opportunity for exploration and for seeking more knowledge of who we are as a spirit essence stuffed inside a human body. And they don't kick you out for asking questions."

Now that I was a board member, we regularly attended twice a month. Rather than just being on the board, my curse of competency and organization skills took over. I organized the church files, alphabetized the bookcase, created a membership database, and assembled a supplemental songbook with modern songs for the Sunday service. By month six, I was burned out. I resigned from the board in July 2003 and walked away.

The takeaway for me was that we are a soul with a body. Not a body with a soul. We are eternal beings having a human experience. The spirit world isn't in the sky. It's all around us. The communication between the living and those in the spirit realm proves the continuation of life, removing our fear of death.

I'll Pray for You!

A FEW YEARS BEFORE MY FATHER passed away, my parents began vacationing every winter for two months in Longboat Key, Florida. When Mom remarried, she and her new husband, Frank, also spent time there. Five years later, Mom, seventy-four, became a widow for the second time, continuing the winter vacation routine by herself.

Longboat Key is an eleven-mile barrier island between Sarasota Bay and the Gulf of Mexico. The bay with a boat dock and fish-cleaning station was behind her condo. The Gulf's white sandy beach across the two-lane Gulf of Mexico Drive was out her front door.

When I flew to Florida to spend a week with Mom, we crossed the road to watch the sunset, sitting on the picnic table under the condo's private hut. As the brilliant red and orange sun descended below the water, Mom said, "And to think we had astronauts that walked up there!"

Huh?

Chuckling, I responded, "Mom! The astronauts walked on the moon. We're looking at the sun."

It took her just a second to realize her error, and then we both roared, laughing about it all week. Another time I visited her, we were walking to the condo with our bucket of fish after casting from the beach when a man from the next building wearing a captain's hat stopped to chat.

"Whatcha catchin', Dottie?"

"Whitefish! Fishing is good today. Paul, this is my daughter, Gaye."

He took my hand with a wink and a sly smile, saying, "You've got a lovely mother."

"Thank you."

Since Mom was the only woman in the condo complex who enjoyed fishing and could clean her own catch, the men were quite smitten with her. I'm sure her long legs, great personality, and the fact that she looked ten years younger than her actual age also influenced their interest.

While chatting with Paul, another man walked up and jokingly said to the captain, "You better be careful around her. She's killed three husbands already!"

Mom's sharp wit immediately came back with, "I have not! I've only killed two."

When Mom was seventy-eight, Ron and I drove to Florida for a visit. We had barely walked in the door when Mom said, "I want you to watch this video and tell me what you think."

The video was of Oprah Winfrey telling an audience that she believes there are many paths to God. When the video ended, Mom asked me, "So, what do you think? Do you believe there are many paths to God?"

The question didn't surprise me. I'd been hiding my nontraditional spiritual exploration from her for years. I assumed the video query was her subtle attempt to determine if I was still a Christian.

Sneaky but impressive move on her part.

If only she hadn't asked me directly, I could have skirted around the answer. I calmed my fear about what she might think about my response and replied, "Yes, I think there are many paths."

"Well!" she snapped. "I'll pray for you!"

Uh oh!

Was I still a Christian? Even I didn't know.

Mom, Ron, and I walked silently as we headed to the beach to watch the sunset. Ron went down to the water's edge while Mom and I settled on the picnic table under the beach hut with our feet planted on the seat like we did every year I visited. This time, instead of light-hearted laughter, the air between us was heavy.

Mom stared out over the waters of the Gulf, saying nothing, and then I heard her quietly speak, "The older I get, the more I think about death."

"Me too," I answered honestly.

"It's important that my girls be with me in heaven."

"I'll be there," I promised. Although my concept of heaven and hell had changed from hers, I knew we would see each other on the other side.

Mom returned to the condo to start dinner when the sun dropped behind the water. As soon as she was out of earshot, I fell apart, sobbing on Ron's good-smelling shirt.

"I can't believe she thinks I'm going to hell just because I believe there's more than one path to God!" I wailed.

We stayed at the beach until I calmed down, twenty to thirty minutes tops. As we returned to the condo, dusk had already blended into night. Mom was heading outside with a flashlight when we reached her door.

With a furious voice, Mom reprimanded, "Where have you been? I've been frantic with worry!"

I'm fifty-five years old, and she's scolding me?

Anger replaced my feeling of loss. I countered with a snotty tone, "I was right where you left me."

"You knew I was coming back here to start dinner. I thought you were right behind me."

My voice was as loud as hers when I shouted, "I was in tears because you think I won't be with you in heaven! You've known me all my life. You know the kind of person I am. Just because I believe there are many paths to God does not mean I'm going to hell!"

This may have been the first time I raised my voice to her. With a shocked face and welling tears, she pulled me into her arms. "I'm sorry. You're right. I'm so sorry."

CHAPTER 27

Unity

IN THE EARLY 2000S, I WAS also a paid guest soloist three or four times a year at Unity of Springfield, Illinois. I didn't care about the money. I missed singing so much that the opportunity to sing for others felt like they were paying me to breathe.

Now that we had no Sunday obligations, we attended Unity regularly.

Don't confuse Unity with Unitarian. They are very similar but not the same.

Unity was birthed in the late nineteenth century during the New Thought Awakening, along with many other metaphysical spiritual movements from that era when America began growing economically, geographically, and educationally with many options for higher education.

With the addition of public lectures and debates available to the general public, higher learning and new thoughts were everywhere: in literature, art, philosophy, history, science, physics, metaphysics, humanity, politics, and religion.

Unity, founded by Charles and Myrtle Fillmore in 1889, became a worldwide spiritual movement—a positive, practical, progressive approach to Christianity based on the teachings of Jesus and the power of affirmative prayer.

Unity has no dogma or creeds. They honor the universal truths in all religions, respect each individual's right to choose a spiritual path, and are an inclusive community. They believe God is absolute good, we are spiritual beings created in God's image, and the spirit of God lives within us; therefore, all people are inherently good.

I saw Unity's concept of God as similar to the Force in the *Star Wars* franchise. A neutral energy without human traits that does not have a favorite religion, country, political party, or football team—a positive power within us that we are to use while in this physical life. "Use the Force, Luke!"

We can call this power God, Universe, Infinite Intelligence, Higher Self, or whatever name rings true.

In Unity, Jesus is recognized as a man, a master teacher, and a way-shower who taught that we all have the Christ Consciousness within us. This was the Jesus I knew, the rebel who taught about love and respect, not someone God sacrificed so I could get a ticket to heaven.

I mean, really? Why would Infinite Intelligence need a human sacrifice? A vengeful, punishing deity goes against everything Jesus taught about God's unconditional love.

Unity's New Thought practical Christianity and positive, empowering messages void of shame, guilt, and judgment resonated so much within me that I knew I had found the spiritual center I'd been searching for.

As I stepped away from traditional Christianity, I felt at peace with my beliefs, but I was still at odds with the Bible being the flawless word of God. I knew that if I shared my current views with others (Mom), I would get a slew of Bible verses tossed at me to prove I was wrong. And that's when the books appeared.

I won't describe each one. The titles say it all: *Misquoting Jesus: The Story Behind Who Changed the Bible and Why* by Bart D. Ehrman, an authority on the history of the New Testament, the early church, and the life of Jesus. *Jesus against*

Christianity: Reclaiming the Missing Jesus, by Jack Nelson-Pallmeyer, Assistant Professor of Justice and Peace Studies at the University of St. Thomas. *The Sins of Scripture: Exposing the Bible's Texts of Hate to Reveal the God of Love*, by retired Episcopal Bishop John Shelby Spong, and one of his many other books, *Why Christianity Must Change or Die: A Bishop Speaks to Believers in Exile*.

Now that I had expert information about how and why there were so many mistakes and alterations in the Bible, I could begin to let go of feeling like I was a believer in exile.

I thoroughly enjoyed Unity's New Thought music, with its positive, encouraging, uplifting Law of Attraction affirmations. Along with singing solos and leading singing, I became part of U4ia, a woman's trio with friends Linda and Veronica, Dwight on the keyboard, and Ron on sound. Rehearsals were super fun as we created our own unique harmonies.

Much of the music the trio sang was complicated for the congregation to join in. I longed to write simple New Thought music. I had the musical skills needed for this, but I didn't play the piano by ear, and I could never get the melodies I heard written down fast enough before they dribbled out of my ear.

Then, my desire to spiritually unfold even more led me to guided meditations by Sanaya Roman and Duane Packer (OrinDaben.com) and a year-long meditation course called Awakening Your Light Body. That was where I realized that when we choose life-affirming thoughts, words, and actions, we experience a more fulfilling and abundant life. Any thought that tells us why we can't have something is an illusion, so we must tell ourselves why we *can* manifest what we want.

I had an immediate epiphany. "I'm not writing music because I keep telling myself I can't."

I knew that wasn't true. I'd written a little jingle in 1973 for a college music class, so why was I doubting myself?

Every day after, I repeated, "I have the skills to write music." Twenty-five days later, I attended a Day of Quiet retreat at the Chiara Center, one of the healing ministries of the Hospital Sisters of St. Francis in Springfield. The Chiara Center replaced the building where I attended all those Walk to Emmaus spiritual retreats.

At the day's end, when we gathered for a final goodbye, a nun closed the day with a short talk. Inspired by her words, a tune jumped into my head. I jotted the words and the basic rhythm in my notebook. As soon as the day concluded, I said a quick goodbye and rushed out the door, repeatedly singing the tune on the drive home.

Dashing into the house, I grabbed the digital recorder I'd just purchased and sang the melody into the recorder. Then I sat down at the piano, listened to the recording, matched the notes on the piano, and put them on staff paper.

I didn't need to learn how to play piano by ear. All I had to do was change my thoughts and record the tune I heard. I added three verses, a chorus, and four-part harmony within a few days. I purchased music notation software and typed the notes into the program. It looked like professional sheet music when it slipped out of the printer. The Unity choir sang it a few weeks later.

Back then, I still had a demanding full-time job working for The American Council of Engineering Companies of Illinois. I was the office manager for eight years and director of administration for ten years. I loved my job, which paid quite well, but as I neared retirement, I longed to let go of business writing to write for myself again.

While cleaning out the basement closet at our new home, I found my 1997 spirit painting in a box with some other stuff I stored when we moved. I read the spirit message I'd taped to the back of the artwork. *DO NOT TARRY! The time is now. Take up the quill as pictured and spread the message of truth, hope, and love to all light beings.*

Oh, no! I've wasted eighteen years!

Then it dawned on me. I'd journaled daily, had over two hundred meditations that I'd used regularly, and read scores of spiritual books. The information I gained over those years was enormous! I was better prepared now to not just write funny stories, but to write a book about my spiritual journey. Too bad I was still overly concerned about what people would think of me once they discovered how far I had traveled from mainstream religion.

So, instead of focusing on blessing hearts, I did what was safe and comfortable. I wrote humorous stories about my life. I set up a Facebook business page and uploaded a few stories. The next step was to push the button and go live.

"Push the button!" Logic said.

I'm not ready!

"Why bother writing stories if you aren't going to share them? Push the damn button!"

Stop pressuring me! I'll do it when I'm ready.

The following weekend, I flew to Oregon for the Orin and DaBen Awakening Your Light Body graduate seminar. My main focus was to show up and bask in three days of spiritual energy. My second goal was to get some insight into my future writing career.

I met Maureen Smith (clearing.org) on the first day. She introduced herself as a hypnotherapist and a published author.

She told me about her books, and I told her about my writing background, my desire to write a book about my spiritual journey, and the four stories waiting in the womb of Facebook for me to push the button so they could enter the world.

The first thing Maureen said was, "Push the button."

Geesh! She's kind of bossy for someone I just met.

I gave her all my arguments. "I'm not sure if I should write humor or spiritual stuff. And I still need to learn how to manage the Facebook page. I don't even know how to get people to find it!"

Maureen was not at all sympathetic to my plight. She calmly said, "Gaye, you're already a published author. You have a book to write about shifting from Christianity to being awakened. It's your book. Spirituality doesn't have to be serious. Go ahead and combine the humor with the spiritual. It will draw people in."

On the last day of the seminar, Maureen confronted me. "I'm going to contact you in a week. If you haven't pushed the button, I will call you daily until you do."

Persistent woman. I really like her.

I pushed the button four days after I got home.

I was going to take time to learn how to manage the Facebook page before inviting people to follow me when my daughter, Karen, called a few minutes later.

Hearing her voice, I gushed, "I just launched my new Facebook writer's page."

Then, without my knowledge or permission, she invited all her friends to my page!

NOOOOOOOOO!

It was too late to panic. What was done was done. With Karen's instruction, I invited all my Facebook friends. By the end of the day, I had over one hundred followers. Watching the numbers rise was beyond thrilling. It was electrifying!

The first story was one of my favorites, titled "Motherhood—It's a Crapshoot!" a humorous story that involved my son Andrew. Three months later, with my son Michael's technology expertise, I also had a website for my writing.

PART THREE

Voicing Myself

I Am the Authority
of Me

Mom was in excellent health, except for the beginning of macular degeneration, when she moved to Springfield at the age of seventy-nine. She'd been living alone in Tennessee for five years. It made sense for her to move back to the Midwest, where her daughters, grandchildren, and great-grandchildren lived.

Mom became very active in an independent living retirement community. She won the Volunteer of the Year award the first year she was there. At the awards ceremony, before announcing the winner, the speaker shared everything the winner had done that year. Mom turned to her neighbor and whispered, "Who in their right mind would do all that?" As soon as the words were out of her mouth, she gasped, "I think they're talking about me!"

With my mother in town, I knew it was time to stop hiding my spiritual life from her, but it was easier said than done. She stayed with us for two weeks while waiting to move into her new apartment. The first Sunday with us, we took her to Unity. I was curious how she would react to "practical" Christianity.

U4ia, the trio I sang in, was scheduled to sing the special music and lead all the congregational songs, which meant I had a perfect view of my mom's face throughout the service. When the trio began to sing the beautiful Celtic Woman's three-part harmony version of "Over the Rainbow," written by Harold Arlen and lyricist Yip Harburg, Mom's eyebrows pinched into a questioning frown.

Uh oh!

I expected this reaction. The song from the movie *The Wizard of Oz* isn't a praise and worship song, but it does have a positive message of believing that dreams can come true.

Mom's eyebrows raised during the meditation when our talented pianist, using his electronic keyboard, created gentle sounds for reflection that mimicked a Native American flute.

Afterward, as we left the building, I asked Mom what she thought about the service. She responded, "I thought the whole congregation was going to levitate out of their seats during that prayer time."

Mom has a unique way of couching her negative observations with humor, leaving me either speechless or laughing. I still giggle when I think of my Unity family slowly rising into the air, bumping their heads on the ceiling!

I enjoyed having her in town—in her own apartment—but she tended to tell me what to do. The weird thing was the backward way she did it.

"You don't want to lose any more weight."

My response was to defend myself. "I'm not trying to lose weight. I'm just eating right."

"Well, you're getting too thin."

"But I feel better when I don't eat junk."

Why am I defending healthy eating?

Then it was my hair: "You don't want your hair any shorter than it is now."

Criminy! I'm now officially a senior citizen, and my mother is telling me how to wear my hair? If I can't stand up to her about these stupid things, how will I ever be honest about my spiritual life?

I thought about the book *Empowering the Spirit: A Process to Activate Your Soul Potential* by Judith Corvin-Blackburn when she wrote, "Our parents decorated our minds in the same way they might have decorated our bedrooms. As we grew older, our interchanges with the rest of society added to the décor of our minds. As you worked with becoming more conscious and with transforming limited beliefs...you stripped the walls bare and can now begin to think about what type of room you wish to create for yourself" (Corvin-Blackburn 2013, 92).

I had already changed my life and beliefs, but figuratively, my mother was still trying to decorate my bedroom. So I wrote a note to myself and stuck it on my kitchen wall, where I would see it every day. It read: "I am the only authority on what is right for me!"

At about that same time, Unity offered a communications course based on the book *The I of the Storm: Embracing Conflict, Creating Peace* by Gary Simmons. The book's first chapter was titled "No One Is against You." The premise is that anything that appears to oppose me has roots within me. In other words, I am the "I" of the storm.

Mom's storm was that she needed me to accept her concept of God so she didn't have to worry that I'd lost my ticket to heaven. My storm was that I wanted my mother to honor who I had become. However, when she asked me to explain my spiritual life, I didn't know what to say. How do I define a spiritual journey that has changed and expanded over a lifetime in a couple of sentences?

For me, it's like an independent study course about what I've learned while living as a human. It's my master's thesis. Maybe I'm writing this book so I don't have to explain myself to anyone.

After Mom moved to Springfield, she wrote her memoir, *Dottie's Delights and Dilemmas*. It was witty, delightfully funny, and an eye-opener for me. I especially like this story:

> "One of my girlfriends had a Ouija board, and when we got together with other friends, they always wanted to find out who they would marry. We would sit there waiting and waiting for the planchette to move, but it never did. I only had so much time to play after school, so I moved it myself. The girls were excited when the spirits talked to them. I wonder what happened when I wasn't there; someone had to move the darn thing."

I'd always suspected Mom was a rebel; now I had proof. She tricked her friends and hid boyfriends from her German father even though he decreed boys were "verboten," a German word meaning "forbidden."

Mom may be overly concerned about breaking God's rules now that she is older, but she is still breaking rules she finds inconvenient. For example, during the Covid-19 pandemic, when her independent living community was on lockdown and no one was allowed to leave their apartment, Mom talked her friends into meeting secretly every afternoon for conversation and wine.

Sneaking out of their apartments, wearing masks while carrying their full glass of wine to the meeting place, these ninety-year-old women would sit six feet apart and lift their masks to sip their Chardonnay, Pinot Grigio, or Cabernet.

One day when Mom and I were together, the conversation turned to God. She told me she knows she can be critical and prays for forgiveness daily. A sense of calm came over me, and

I knew what to say this time. "Mom, for just a moment, set the Bible aside." I moved my hands to the right to visualize pushing the Bible away.

"And leave behind everything you've learned about God and Jesus from other people." I pushed invisible people to my left.

"Now, look into your own heart. What would your life be like if you believed God gave you the freedom to live any way you want without fear of eternal punishment?"

Mom's eyes lit up like a child's seeing presents under the Christmas tree for the first time. As her mind filled with possibilities, a big grin appeared on her face. She raised her hands to her cheeks, whispering, "Oh my! Oh my!"

Then she shook her head and thrust both hands palm forward. "No. No. I wasn't raised to believe that way. I can't do this. I'm sorry."

My heart filled with unconditional love for her as she said no to the possibility of a faith without fear. It was her choice. We each create our own lives, and there is no right or wrong way. With that thought, I knew I no longer needed my mom's approval. My bedroom was finally my own.

CHAPTER 29

Speak Up, Dammit!

I MET JYLL HOYRUP, AN AMERICAN living in Belize, in an online Zoom writing group led by Judy McNutt, a holistic writing coach (judymcnutt.com). Jyll would show up with her sun-kissed skin in a swimsuit-like top, blonde hair, and a tie-dyed wall hanging, gently blowing in the breeze. She always looked relaxed and at peace while I was freezing my ass off in Illinois, wearing fleece-lined leggings under my sweatpants, two pairs of socks, and a long-sleeved shirt under a sweatshirt.

I was impressed with Jyll's writing and fun demeanor and a little jealous of what looked like a tranquil lifestyle. When she shared a story she wrote about listening to her intuition and leaving a good job in Seattle, Washington, to move to Belize, I had to know more and reached out to her through Facebook Messenger.

Jyll is an intuitive energy healer, master psychic, and coach (jyllhoyrup.com) who helps those who are awakening to become more aligned with their soul's purpose, tap into their soul wisdom (i.e., intuition), and eliminate blocks, beliefs, and patterns that are holding them back in their life. Jyll is the author of *Rock Your Intuition: A Practical Guide to Understanding and Using Your Intuition*.

Energy medicine has been around for thousands of years. Everything is made up of energy. If you sit still and focus on your body, you can feel the energy within you. Some call it vibrations. The Universe is all energy and vibration.

When our energy/vibration is balanced, we feel good, excited, calm, and confident! When it's out of balance. We say things like: "I'm out of sorts. I'm stressed. I'm frustrated. I'm bored."

I joined Jyll's free Facebook group and regularly attended her weekly "Zap-It-Up" live event to magnify my intentions. One time, I mentioned in the chat that I'd had coughing issues since I was a young child, and usually, once a year, I'd get a cold followed by a dry choking cough that lasts for at least six weeks. I told her, "I've been coughing for five months, yet this time I never had a cold."

Jyll responded, "Louise Hay says that a cough is a desire to bark at the world and say, 'Listen to me!'" Louise Hay is an author who founded Hay House Publishing at age sixty.

Jyll's words made sense, given my history of not speaking up. I immediately scheduled a healing session. Before it began, Jyll commented, "I find it interesting that you were starting to get more into your writing routine and expressing yourself, and now you're coughing. It almost feels like you are thwarting your own efforts, but it's all subconscious and energetic. It's not like you're doing it on purpose."

"The other thing," Jyll added, "is the throat chakra is all about communication, self-expression, and creativity. (Chakras are seven swirling wheels of energy that correspond to nerve centers and major organs in the body.) I'm sensing that this is a big roadblock for you, and I feel like it's tied to ancestral females on your mother's side. When it's ancestral, it's literally in your DNA, an innate part of who you are."

Jyll paused, closing her eyes for a moment. "Okay, I'm getting that it goes back nineteen generations. What we do today will tie into a current dynamic with your mom. You haven't lived in her house for years, but these energetic ties and this ancestral pattern still exist."

I had to chuckle. I wasn't expecting Mom to be involved, but it didn't surprise me either. Jyll closed her eyes again. "You have eleven past lives for this issue. They're also all female, which is unusual. The past lives and generations of ancestral women tell me this is a big pattern you have had in many of your lives. Shifting this is going to be huge for you."

When the session ended, Jyll added, "You're blossoming and branching out. You're breaking fear, and it's a whole new up-level in a book you'll write. It's like turning a corner for you to own your life. You're going to be shining in the world, and you're going to be doing it in a way where everyone can relate."

Jyll didn't know I had folders of notes I was saving for the day I'd start writing about my spiritual journey. I started the file after removing the spirit painting from my basement. I appreciated her words of confidence, but a book needs an ending, and I didn't have one.

Jyll wasn't finished. "If you think about what happened in these past generations and lives, there's a theme of female powerlessness. I feel these were all very strong women, but they couldn't express themselves in the world due to the times in which they lived. They're telling me this isn't just you, so don't beat yourself for not speaking up, creating boundaries, and not being true to yourself when you first became a minister's wife."

She paused again. "Interesting. They're saying you're going to be—voicing yourself. I've not heard that before; usually, I hear, 'You're going to speak your truth.' Hmmm. Voice yourself. I like that. There could be a story for you coming from this."

"They're showing me you, reaching down into the depths of your gut—voicing yourself. You might write a little different way, more passionate or heartfelt. I know you write humor, but maybe there is a time for the tender, too. I'm seeing things coming up deep within you."

I liked the phrase "Voice yourself." It reminded me of the slogan for a diamond ad campaign in one of my favorite movies, *How to Lose a Guy in 10 Days*. The tagline was "Ladies, frost yourself!" In other words, don't wait for a man to give you diamonds; buy them for yourself.

I shared the ancestral healing session with Mom a few days later and was surprised by her response. "That makes sense." She said, "My mother never spoke up to my dad. As for me, I've always felt that I could have done so much more with my life if I'd had the chance."

We had a heartfelt open conversation about how we clam up when the other brings up spirituality or religion because we are afraid we might say something to alienate the other.

Mom's concern about my spiritual life has caused me to scrutinize every spiritual concept I've embraced. I count her among the many women who have assisted me in my spiritual journey.

A month later, my friend Ellen, who encouraged me to join Judy McNutt's writing group, also introduced me to Anne Aleckson's SuperSelf Academy (annealeckson.info).

Anne is a modern mystic and spiritual guide who lives in Australia. She helps people manifest and channel their unique genius through practical, quick, and simple modern spiritual practices so they can be, do, and have it all. Her signature line was, "Be the change to see the change," meaning that if you want to see love in the world, you have to be love in the world.

Anne's message, her genuine smile, and her delightful

Aussie accent brought me into another spiritual expansion.

I'd been saying, "Life happens for me" for many years, but when Anne first said the phrase, she added, "And you can't get it wrong."

Oh my gosh! I can't get life wrong!

And to think I'd lived my entire life with indecision because I feared making wrong choices. My mind was suddenly calm and clear. Life happens for me; I can't get it wrong.

Woo-hoo!

The next topic was self-love. I thought I had this in the bag until Anne said, "We are not loving ourselves when we have negative thoughts about who we are."

Gasp!

I now recognized that a harsh critic lived in my head. The joy I felt when I thought about writing a book would plummet into oblivion as soon as the critic started saying things like, "What makes you think you can write a book? You're not good enough. What if people don't like what you have to say? What will you do when those darts start flying? You're not ready for this. You don't even have an ending." Its brutal reviews even made Positive Pollyanna run away and hide.

Working with Anne was a game changer. I wrote down what I felt were the five most important concepts I learned from her and turned them into first-person affirmations. When I shared them with her, she suggested I put them to music because words are easier to remember when sung.

"That's a good idea," I replied, quickly dismissing it. I only wrote music when inspired, and my focus for the year was to start writing the book—as soon as I got the ending. As I opened my eyes the following morning, I heard the melody for those five affirmations.

Where's my phone? Where's my phone?! I have to record the tune before I lose it!

I hopped out of bed, sang the melody into my iPhone, and after figuring out the notes, I added them to my music software. I needed to tweak a few lyrics to fit the melody and add harmony, but that was all. Receiving music through inspiration and having it pop into my head is exhilarating! I get fully engrossed in making music. Time seems to stand still, and for the most part, the critic is quiet.

When I shared the first draft with Anne, she was tickled pink. "When you're ready, would you make a video singing it and share it in our private Facebook group?"

"I'd be happy to." The words spilled out before the critic screamed, "A video? That's a lot of work. You're not ready."

I affirmed that life happens for me; I can't get it wrong. And the pesty bugger disappeared.

The song took a week to finish. I kept second-guessing my editing and wasted most of the week fiddling with it, only to realize when I was all done that it was back to the same version I'd had on day three.

It took another week to videotape myself singing. I had to find a place to record in the house with good lighting that didn't reflect onto my glasses, pick a colorful background, and try on every piece of clothing in my closet before choosing what to wear.

I was still a bit uneasy about posting the video until I had a dream. I was at a retreat center in a remote wooded area with a dozen people when the big-game hunter from the original *Jumanji* movie arrived with his Winchester M1901 lever-action shotgun at the ready.

Terrified, I hid behind a tree. The next time he appeared, I crouched behind a Model T automobile on the dirt floor of a shed. The last time, I hid in a kitchen cabinet in the retreat center. With my nose smashed between my knees, I asked myself, "Where will I go the next time he arrives? The dishwasher? Behind a shower curtain? If this is my last night on Earth, I don't want to spend it afraid."

Untangling my body from the cabinet, I headed for the library, picked a book off the shelf, and settled on the sofa to enjoy a good read. Accepting my fate, I sat unruffled and unafraid as the hunter entered the library.

His thundering voice reverberated off the vaulted ceiling when he threatened, "There you are. You can't escape from me now!" Halting in front of me with his rifle pointed at my heart, he silently waited.

Composed and at peace with whatever would happen next, I lifted my chin and stared boldly into his eyes. His glare softened for a moment before he nodded and walked away. And then, I knew—he didn't want me. He was hunting fear, but I had none to give.

I posted the song "Life is Happening for Me" on two of Anne's Facebook group pages the following day. She responded, "When you're ready, post it to your personal Facebook page, too."

Drat!

She wasn't going to let this go until I put myself out there in front of friends and family. It was like Maureen repeatedly telling me to "push the button."

I posted the video a few days later. It got good reviews. No one questioned the lyrics, said it wasn't good enough, or threw darts. The action of voicing myself in public without fear bolstered my confidence.

I Know Who I Am

THE FIRST TIME MOM HEARD THE New Thought songs I wrote for Unity, I expected an enthusiastic *I'm so proud of you* response, but instead, I got an understated *nice*. Was it the melody, the lyrics, or the simplicity of the music she didn't like? After that reaction, I would mention I wrote another song, but I didn't sing it for her or give any details, and she didn't ask.

Then, one day, she surprised me as I sat with her in her doctor's waiting room. "Tell me about your new song."

"Okay! It's a little jingle called 'Life Is Happening for Me.'"

Life is happening for me. I can't get it wrong.

When I ask, it's always given.

I'm more than enough to see my dreams come true,

When I live in my highest vibration,

For I'm a physical manifestation of All-That-Is.

"But the song is all about you?" she replied.

"That's because it's an affirmation song. When we say positive statements to ourselves, it changes our negative thoughts into positive ones."

We were both sitting in silence when I had an aha moment. I didn't have to defend my music, beliefs, hair, or diet to anyone. And then I knew exactly what to say, but since the waiting room was packed with people, I trusted a better opportunity to speak would show up later in the day. I was a little nervous, but I let it go. Life happens for me; I can't get it wrong. Right?

After lunch, Mom mentioned a pianist she'd recently heard, giving me a perfect segway. "Speaking of music, Mom, God gives me the music I write. I don't know why he doesn't give me praise and worship songs, but he doesn't. I write what I'm given and trust God knows what he's doing."

"What does physical whatever mean?" she asked.

"A physical manifestation of 'All-That-Is' means that we are an expression of God. The Kingdom of God is within."

"Why don't you just say you're an expression of God?"

"There must be many people in the world who need to hear those particular words, or God would not have given them to me."

"Well, I'm not going to change what I believe," she replied.

"That isn't my intent," I said truthfully.

I learned two things from this conversation. When I speak with confidence and self-assurance instead of hemming, hawing, and hiding, there is nothing to fear, and the words that need to be said will be there. The other thing was, why didn't I let God take the blame sooner?

A few days later, I woke up early, fully awake. I got out of bed, settled into a comfy chair, and listened to a guided meditation called "Manifesting Your Writing." The instructions were to visualize the energy I wanted to create, such as imagining it as a pattern, color, symbol, or object of pure energy.

Every time I used this meditation, I would get stuck at the suggestion of a pattern and kept visualizing a green and red plaid kilt worn by a heavyset man playing the bagpipes with his bare knees poking out above his socks. This wasn't an image I wanted to contemplate.

Get out of my head!

So, I thought, "What I want is for my writing to flow from inspiration like how I write music. What would that look like?"

I envisioned a cool, clean mountain stream nestled among tall trees reaching up to a clear blue sky reflecting itself in the water that flowed effortlessly around rocks and boulders.

At first, I thought the stones symbolized challenges in my life until I remembered nothing can stop rushing water. It's so powerful—it created the Grand Canyon! If I genuinely believed that life happens for me and I couldn't get it wrong, no obstacles could stop me.

I'd been flowing over and around every challenge that came my way since I was eighteen. Occasionally, I still sat on the pity potty, but only for a few minutes before releasing the problem to allow the solution to appear. Perhaps this spiritual journey had actually fulfilled my desire to *be* Pollyanna.

A memory then arose. I'm thirty years old, sitting on the sofa, trying to stay awake at the crack of dawn while reading the Bible, when I hear, "Go back to bed, find out who you are, and then you'll know Me."

Holy Ka Moly! I know who I am. I am an eternal soul having a human experience. I am one with God, The Universe, Infinite Intelligence, All-That-Is, the Force, etc. I can't get life wrong because I am the authority over who I want to be and what I want to do and believe while vacationing on planet Earth.

I leaped off my chair and started dancing throughout the house, saying over and over, "I KNOW WHO I AM! I KNOW WHO I AM!"

Oh my gosh! Knowing who I am is the ending of my book. "IT'S TIME TO WRITE THE BOOK."

Empowering confidence energized every cell in my body, and I declared, "I AM GOING TO WRITE THE BOOK—NOW."

As soon as I heard Ron rattling about in the kitchen, I rushed in to regale him with what happened while he slept.

"I know who I am! I'm ready to write my memoir," I gushed.

Ron has always supported whatever I wanted to do with my life. He smiled and calmly said, "Okay." Then he put his arms around me, whispering, "I love you."

"I love you too!"

As I turned to leave the kitchen, I thought I heard him say something and looked back to see him dancing, shaking his booty, mumbling, "I married a cheerleader who's gonna be an author!"

What is it with guys and their cheerleader fixation?

The next day, I saw an announcement that Ashley Mansour, the LA Writing Coach, would hold a two-day free webinar based on her book *The Writer's Success Code: 7-Day Action Guide*, which I had downloaded and read three months earlier. I signed up for the webinar without hesitation.

After the event, I immediately scheduled a consultation. Two weeks later, we were working together. Ninety days after that, the first draft of this book manifested into physical form. I should have been excited, but I couldn't grasp the magnitude of what I had accomplished.

The warm August day and cloudless sky lured me outside for a walk. I listened to golden oldies music through my earbuds, and when the Beach Boys sang "Good Vibrations," I had an epiphany. I'd spent years thinking about writing this book. The vibration of expectation was so ingrained in me that I couldn't accept the truth of success.

When my neighbor passed by, saying, "Good morning. How are you?" I answered, "I just finished writing the first draft of a memoir about my spiritual journey."

And with that verbal public announcement, the vibration of achievement stepped in to take its rightful place.

CHAPTER 31

Turn on Your Lights

I'VE COME A LONG WAY FROM that naïve teenager who was tossed unprepared and unqualified into the role of minister's wife. I got married because I thought I would miss something if I didn't. That something has been an amazing adventure of self-realization.

From today's perspective, my life has unfolded perfectly. I've learned that I can't change anyone but myself, self-love isn't the same thing as being selfish, reading books that challenge and introduce me to new ideas expands my mind, and if I want to be heard, I have to voice myself without fear.

Every journey is a process: We explore, grow in knowledge, release what no longer defines us, and embrace what feels right. Our journey is never finished; no matter how much we awaken, there's always more awakening to experience.

The concepts that I've shared in this book are *my* truths. My intent has not been to dismiss anyone's religion, for it has a place in our lives as a diving board into the spirit world. But we must ask ourselves, "Do I want my physical and spiritual life to include fear or joy?"

If we want to be heard, we must let go of fear. I once dreamed that Ron and I were hosting a party in the country surrounded by cornfields at a house that didn't belong to us. He was outside by the campfire, regaling a few of our guests with his Navy stories. I was in the kitchen, chatting with friends, nibbling from the veggie tray, and readying the food for the cookout.

I stepped outside to see if our other guests had arrived, but they hadn't. The sun had set. The moon was just a sliver, and most stars had not yet appeared. It was extremely dark except for the light coming from the small campfire. I hollered into the dark expanse. "Ron! Turn on the stadium lights! How will people find us if the lights aren't on?"

When I woke from the dream, I recognized the dream's location was at the *Field of Dreams* movie site in Iowa, which we had recently visited. Once we exited the highway, getting to the site was another six miles of right and left turns on mostly gravel roads surrounded by cornfields. Our guests would never have found our location in the dark without the stadium lights—unless they were part bat.

We have a choice. We can continue hiding who we have become or turn on our stadium lights so we are seen and heard. What will you choose?

> *Life happens for us.*
> *We can't get it wrong.*
> *When we ask, it's always given.*
> *We are more than enough to see our dreams come true,*
> *When we live in our highest vibration,*
> *For we ARE a manifestation of All-That-Is.*

Afterword

MY CHILDREN ARE IN THEIR FORTIES. Since they are each the authority over what is best for them, my job as their mother is to love them unconditionally and get out of their way.

My mother is in her nineties and still worries that I won't be with her in heaven, but that doesn't stop us from laughing whenever we are together.

Donn went on to teach music in public schools and colleges. After retirement, he returned to local church ministry. He also serves on the United Methodist District Committee on Ministry, which allows him to dialogue with new ministers. He shares our story as an example of what not to do.

Acknowledgments

FIRST, I MUST THANK MY HUSBAND, Ron, for his unconditional love and support. For buying TV headphones so I wouldn't be lured from my writing desk into the living room to waste time watching a movie, and for food magically appearing on my desk when the words were flowing.

Thank you to Crystal Hodge, who I called at least once a week while writing the book, when I needed help finding the right words for what I was trying to say and for being one of my beta readers, along with Virginia Carlson, Jyll Hoyrup, Casey Hutchison, Ken Mitchell, Don O'Neal, and Alyssa Furling. Thank you to Ashley Mansour, the LA Writing Coach, without whose guidance this book would never have been written or published, and to all those who have assisted me in my spiritual journey; authors and friends, mentioned and not mentioned, including the well-intentioned dragons.

Most importantly, I thank my family and friends for the joy of having each of them in my life.

Sources

Burroughs, H. Gordon. *Becoming a Spiritualist*. Port City Press, 1962, page 15.

Corvin-Blackburn, Judith. *Empowering the Spirit: A Process to Activate Your Soul Potential*. Healing Concept Publishing, 2013, page 92.